Money and Debt:

A Solution to the Global Crisis

Thomas H. Greco, Jr.

Second Edition 1990

First edition published February, 1989
Revised August, 1989

Thomas H. Greco, Jr., Publisher
P.O. Box 42663
Tucson, AZ 85733

Additional copies may be obtained for $6.50 each plus $1.50 for postage and handling.

ISBN 0-9625208-1-0

Table of Contents

Preface

This book began as a compilation of three essays which I wrote during 1988, and which I have since revised several times. These essays comprise Parts I, II, and III. They express ideas which have been slowly taking form over the past nine years, a time during which I have focused much of my attention on fundamental research into the subjects of money and exchange.

Although I have an extensive academic background in management, finance and quantitative analysis, the understanding of economics which I gained through formal study within academia was superficial, narrowly focused and, for the most part based on premises which are questionable at best and in many cases erroneous. From the beginning, my research has been problem-centered and motivated by a growing awareness of the deepening and interrelated global problems of both human and ecological degradation, a strong desire to understand the root causes of these problems and the hope that out of these efforts might come some clues which might lead to a remedy.

The process of this research has been one of spontaneous development involving a network of numerous correspondents. I determined early-on that the orthodox economic academy had little to offer in terms of penetrating problem-centered analysis and that I would have to look elsewhere for insights powerful enough to bear fruit. For this reason I have cultivated colleagues who are for the most part extra-academic scholars and activists, and sought out materials from a broad range of religious and political, as well as academic perspectives, often finding grains of truth in what might otherwise have been discarded as biased or sectarian rhetoric. I discovered a wealth of valuable material which had been forgotten, overlooked or obscured.

I soon came to realize that the problems which we seek to solve derive from structural deficiencies and foundational flaws in many of the dominant institutions, and I concluded that only a thoroughgoing restructuring would bring about an effective solution - restructuring in not only economic matters, but throughout the whole of what we call civilization.

This work is the product of many minds. What I have tried to do is to synthesize their diverse thoughts into a coherent matrix which might begin to demystify for the ordinary reader the subject of money and global finance, and to lay out a framework for what I think to be a liberative approach to money and exchange. However, although the primary focus here is on economics, these questions cannot be adequately dealt with apart from the broader context of the social structure within which they operate. I hope in a later volume to address these matters more adequately so that the reader can gain an understanding of the attitudinal changes and sociological shifts necessary to bring the world through its current crisis.

I am greatly indebted to my many mentors and colleagues, and to all those friends, relatives and associates through whom Divine providence has supported these efforts. May our work continue, and may it bear fruit in the form of a more healthy, happy and peaceful world in which life may prosper and humankind, in unity, may fulfill its destiny.

Introduction

The first part of this book is based on a presentation which I made at the Seventh Assembly of the Fourth World which was sponsored by the School of Living and held in Raleigh, NC in August 1988. This part deals with an analysis of the current monetary and financial situation and shows that there are fundamental flaws which during the present century have manifested in recurrent and alternating recession and inflation and, more recently, in "stagflation", and now in an explosion of debt worldwide.

Unlike most other analyses which have been published, this one examines the basic structure of the global monetary system, shows how it is intimately linked to debt and government finances, and identifies the engine which drives the debt explosion. It includes what I consider to be a reasonable proposal for settlement of the international debt crisis, which could, if the political will existed to implement it, quickly transform this strife-torn world.

Following the Assembly, in an effort to answer more completely numerous questions which had been raised about my proposed approaches to a solution, I went to work on Parts II and III. Part II considers the nature of money and its role in the exchange process, the problem of value measurement and the characteristics of an ideal money. It attempts to summarize and extend the work of that monetary genius, E. C. Riegel. Part III examines the confusions which result from legal provisions such as "legal tender" and banking practices which force money to serve conflicting purposes. In it, I argue that the functions which money is said to serve should be segregated. I also make what I believe to be a novel proposal for a global objective "value" standard. In this, the second edition, I have made extensive revisions to Part I and have substantially enlarged and elaborated Part III. Part II, except for the correction of a few typographical errors and one clarifying change in terminology, remains much the same.

The general acclaim with which the first edition was greeted was very gratifying and has provided me encouragement in my further efforts to help demystify the subjects of money and finance for the general population. I am also grateful to many of my network colleagues for their extensive and specific criticisms which I hope have made this edition a substantial improvement over the previous one.

In light of some of the reactions to the first edition, I see a need to clarify several points. These are things which were at least implicit in the body of the text but which appear not to have come through to some readers as strongly as I had intended. First of all, I believe that "the end is inherent in the means" and I therefore advocate nothing but voluntary and non-violent action in bringing about change. Secondly, I believe that monopoly and special privilege established by law are ultimately harmful to all, even those who ostensibly benefit therefrom. I, therefore, favor the elimination of all such legal statutes by means provided for in the Constitution of the United States and established in American tradition. Thirdly, I believe in the sovereignty of the individual person and the rule of conscience, and that no state authority has the right to conscript either his/her person or property. Fourthly, I favor free and unencumbered experimentation with exchange mechanisms, including alternative currencies and barter and reciprocal trade associations, "value" standards, accounting units and cooperative ownership structures, and voluntary choice in using any of them. Finally, in keeping with the foregoing, I do not advocate government prohibitions of usury or any other financial practices. Rather, I favor the withdrawal of government from the marketplace and the elimination of statutes which allow some to have unfair advantage over others. When there are truly free markets to provide buyers and sellers with alternatives, and contracts are entered into voluntarily, there will be no need for restrictive regulation by government.

Money and Debt: A Solution to the Global Crisis

Part I - Political Money and the Debt Imperative: Why the Budget Can't Be Balanced

The Debt Crisis

The whole world today seems to be awash in a sea of debt which threatens to drown us all. Many Third World countries, despite their huge increases in production for export, are unable to pay even the interest due on their accumulated indebtedness to Western banks and governments. In the U. S., the levels of both public (government) and private debt are increasing at alarming rates. The Federal budget deficits of recent years far exceed anything thought possible just a decade ago. Why is this happening and why is it a problem? In order to understand that, one must first understand some financial facts of life.

The "Magic" of Compound Interest

Suppose you were to deposit a single dollar in a bank account which pays 6 percent annual interest. After one year your account balance would have grown to $1.06, a modest sum and nothing to get very excited about. If you left that amount intact, by the end of the second year, your balance would be a bit over $1.123. After three years, your balance would be $1.191. And so on, each year the principal would be increasing, so the amount of interest earned would increase. Over a period of a few years, the amounts do not seem startling; still, your deposit balance would double in about 12 years. And it would continue to double every 12 years. In just 30 years you would have 5.74 times your original amount. Still, in absolute terms, these amounts do not seem very large. Over a longer time frame however, it is a different story. In 100 years, a single dollar grows to be $339.30. Suppose your great grandmother had made a deposit of $100 one hundred years ago, to be left for her descendents today. If she had done that you would be the inheritors of the tidy sum of almost thirty four thousand dollars. If your great great great grandmother had done the same two hundred years ago, you and the other members of your family would share a family fortune of over 11.5 million dollars.

Still more startling are the figures which would prevail if the rate of interest had been ten percent per annum. At that rate, a single dollar grows to $13,780.65 in one hundred years. Great grandma's foresight in investing one hundred dollars would have rewarded you with a legacy of almost 1.4

million dollars, and great great great grandma's legacy (after 200 years) would be an unbelievable 18.9 billion dollars (that's right, billion). One would not think that such modest sums could grow at such modest rates to become such enormous amounts. Such is the magic of compound interest.

Table A shows the figures for growth at compound interest up through 270 years. It will be noted that at 6% per annum interest, the amount grows by a factor of 1.76 every 10 years; at 10%, it grows by a factor of 2.59 every 10 years. Figure 1 shows this growth graphically. It can be seen that the curves accelerate upward, shooting more rapidly toward infinity as time goes on. Such mathematical relationships are known as exponential functions.

What has all this to do with reality? Unfortunately, it has far too much to do with reality. Interest rates of 6% and 10% are well within the range of actual practice - consider savings accounts paying 6% or 7%, prime bank rates of 9% to 10%, mortgage rates of 11% to 14% and credit card rates of 18% to 24% or more. Is it reasonable to expect such conditions to continue indefinitely? In nature, exponential growth is always temporary; it either levels off or collapses.

The Long-term Growth of Debt

Figure 2 shows the total public and private debt for the United States from 1916 to 1976 as reported by the U. S. government. This includes the debts of all levels of government, businesses and consumers. It can be seen that this curve looks remarkably similar to the compound interest curves of Figure 1. Figure 3 shows the same information plotted on a logarithmic scale. An exponential function plotted on such a scale shows as a straight line, the slope of which represents the growth rate. It will be noted that the growth rates were slower in some periods and faster in others. It can be seen that the rate of growth was higher than normal during the war years of the teens and the forties, due presumably to heavy government borrowing to finance the wars, and during the Depression years of the thirties, the total debt actually declined. But over the entire period of 60 years, it can be shown that the total debt grew at an average annual rate of about 6.6%. This rate of growth far exceeds the rate of inflation of the currency, population growth, or growth in real output of the economy.

Robert Blain estimates that total debt amounted to only 28% of Gross National Product (GNP) in 1790 ("United States Public and Private Debt: 1791 to 2000", *International Social Science Journal,* UNESCO, November, 1987. Paris). Total debt was 170% of GNP in 1916, 213% in 1976, and 227% in 1984. These data suggest that there is some sort of debt imperative built into the financial structure, and indeed there is, as we shall see.

Table A

FUTURE VALUE OF ONE DOLLAR
AT COMPOUND INTEREST

AFTER YEAR	AT 6% PER ANNUM	AT 10% PER ANNUM
1	1.0600	1.1000
2	1.1236	1.2100
3	1.1910	1.3310
4	1.2625	1.4641
5	1.3382	1.6105
6	1.4185	1.7716
7	1.5036	1.9487
8	1.5938	2.1436
9	1.6895	2.3579
10	1.7908	2.5937
20	3.2071	6.7275
30	5.7434	17.4494
40	10.2856	45.2593
50	18.4201	117.3910
60	32.9875	304.4821
70	59.0757	789.7483
80	105.7955	2,048.405
90	189.4636	5,313.035
100	339.3002	13,780.65
110	607.6346	35,743.46
120	1,088.181	92,709.36
130	1,948.765	240,464.2
140	3,489.939	623,702.5
150	6,249.946	1,617,724.
160	11,192.69	4,195,961.
170	20,044.40	10,883,240.
180	35,896.45	28,228,340.
190	64,285.03	73,217,060.
200	115,124.60	189,906,200.
210	206,170.6	492,568,000.
220	369,219.9	1,277,595,000.
230	661,216.3	3,313,753,000.
240	1,184,137.	8,595,024,000.
250	2,120,608.	22,293,280,000.
260	3,797,684.	57,823,050,000.
270	6,801,069.	149,978,100,000.

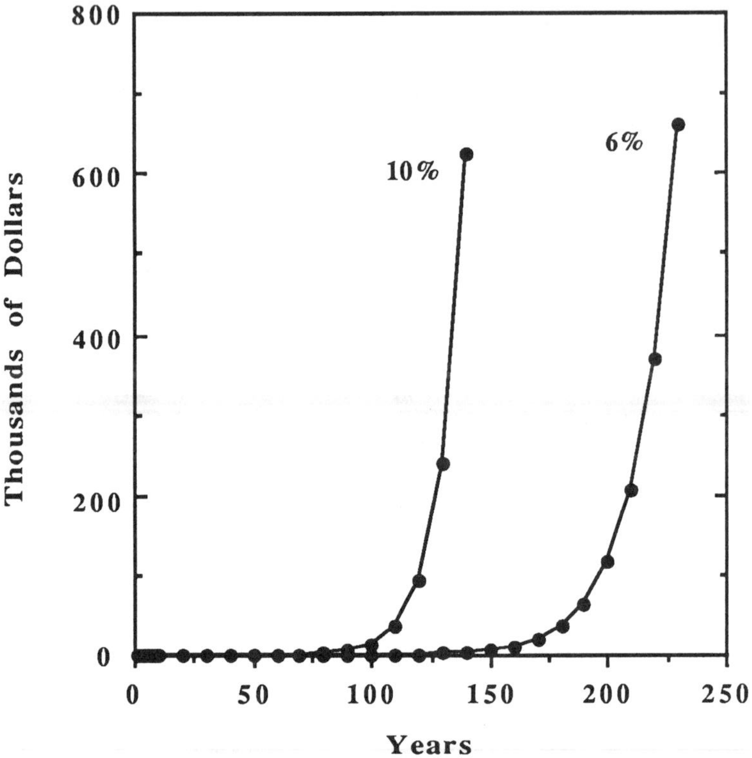

Figure 1. Growth of one dollar at compound interest.

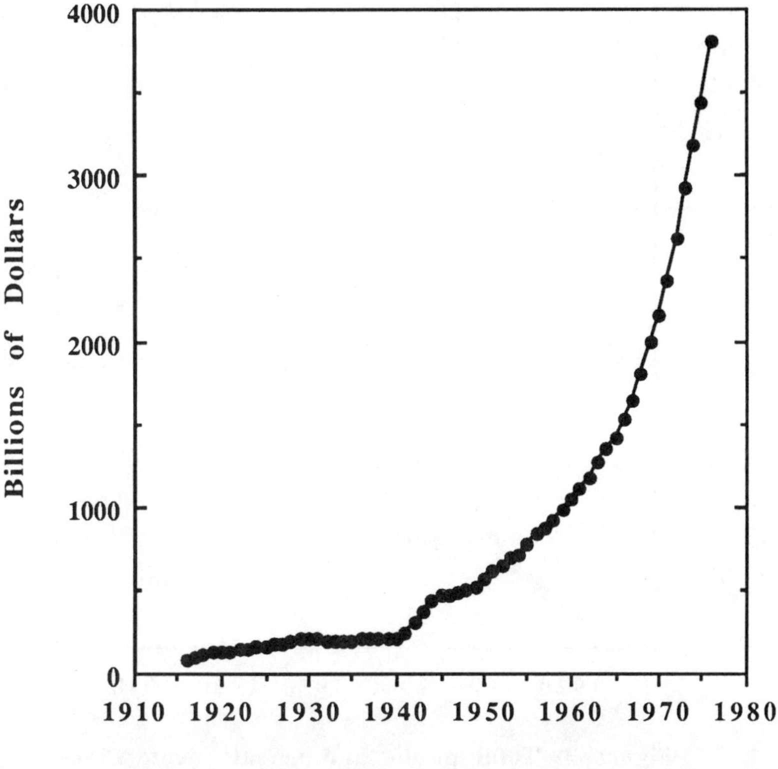

Figure 2. Total public and private debt, 1916-76.

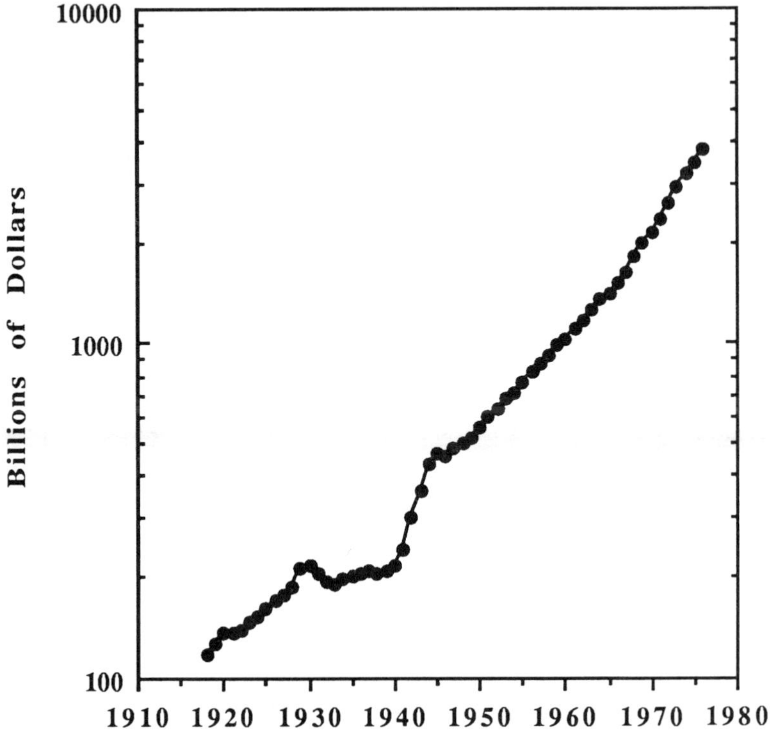

Figure 3. Total public and private debt, 1916-76. (Logarithmic scale)

Why the Federal Budget Cannot Be Balanced

One facet of the debt crisis which is getting increasing attention of late is the Federal government debt and the deficits which have become an inevitable and increasing part of the Government's budgets. At last, even some orthodox economists and financial experts are saying that there is a limit to how large the Federal debt can get and that something must be done to stem the pattern of ever-increasing budget deficits. The most notable recent action which has been taken by Congress and the President is the Gramm-Rudman Law, which calls for automatic spending reductions if the Congress and the President are not able to meet certain deficit targets over time. This is equivalent to your typical New Year's resolutions, well intended but not likely to make any real difference. It simply does not address the causes of the problem.

Budgetary problems, in general, reduce to the consideration of the two fundamental factors which comprise a budget - revenues and expenditures. A deficit is simply the result of expenditures exceeding revenues. The logical process for reducing a budget deficit, the one ordinarily followed by businesses and other organizations, is to 1) increase revenues, 2) reduce expenditures, or both. Simple and straight-forward. Why, then, is it not possible for the Federal government to eliminate its budget deficits? Those who practice the "art" of politics will answer that revenues cannot be increased because the people dislike taxes and will resist attempts to increase them beyond a certain amount. And so it is. At the same time, the people demand services from the government, and each Representative is intent on looking good to his/her constituents. Again, true. Indeed, except for the "pork barrel", by which politicians feed the popular illusion that the state is the great benefactor of the people, and the pervasive wish to get something for nothing, the establishment of true grass-roots democracy should have long since become reality.

The Central Government - Central Bank Nexus

What people forget is that government can, at best, only give back to the people what it has taken from the people. The Federal budget is a grand redistribution system designed to take from some and give to others. The obvious and highly touted expenditures for welfare and social programs are but a minimal part of this redistribution, intended to feed the popular myth. By far, the greatest amounts go, not to the poor and disadvantaged, nor to popular social uses, but to various fiefdoms of privilege which have been established in various ways, including, first and foremost, the banking and financial cartel, the "military-industrial complex", the entrenched bureaucracy and special interests with friends in high places.

But this is not the root of the matter. If all were visible and above board, the various political difficulties in reducing spending or increasing revenues could be overcome if the will were actually there to do it and the people were allowed to make their own choices. In order to understand the magnitude of the problem, one must examine it from a different level, one which exposes the interconnections which exist between government finance and the monetary system.

Few people understand that this interconnection exists, much less how it operates. But once this is understood, it becomes obvious that a balanced Federal budget would spell disaster for the economy as it is presently structured. The money supply would shrink and business would grind to a halt. The subsequent depression would be awesome. Why? In order to understand that, one must first understand the nature of the present monetary system and how it operates.

Some Relevant History

Money, and the role of the government with respect to money, have been recurrent issues throughout our nation's history since colonial times. The study of this history is extremely enlightening in helping to understand not only the economic picture, but the whole panorama of historical events. Some notable episodes are Andrew Jackson's confrontation with the international banking cartel (Jackson called them "a den of vipers") over the re-establishment of a central bank (the Bank of the United States), Abraham Lincoln's issuance of currency (called "greenbacks") directly by the Treasury, which saved the cost of interest and enraged the bankers, President James Garfield's insistence that the government honor its obligation by redeeming the "greenbacks" in gold at full face value, William Jennings Bryan's "Cross of Gold" speech, and the secret maneuverings which led up to the passage of the Federal Reserve Act in 1913.

Central Banks

In the United States, the central bank is known as the Federal Reserve System. It's name implies that it is an agency of the Federal government, but in actuality, it is independent of the government, is controlled by a handful of international financiers and operates for the benefit of its members, the banks. It is actually a cartel which has increasingly tightened its grip on all monetary and financial matters within the United States, and is a key link in a global network of central banks which controls commerce world-wide. (For an excellent history and description of the Federal Reserve see Murray Rothbard's "The Federal Reserve As a Cartelization Device" in *Money in Crisis*,Pacific Institute For Policy Studies, San Francisco, 1984).

Interest and Usury

There is a difference between interest and usury but the distinction has been obscured. Because of its negative connotations deriving from religious prohibitions against its practice, the term "usury" has all but ceased to be mentioned. There is no telling when or where the practice of usury originated but it has been a subject of recurrent controversy and debate for at least three thousand years. It is prominently mentioned in the Bible, in the Koran and in Canon law. All of these prescribe severe punishments for its practice. Why, then, has the giving and taking of interest (usury) become standard practice, and why are almost all of us participants in it? Unfortunately, most of the historical arguments relating to the practice of usury were not based on economic analysis, but rather, seemed to come from a perspective which tried to second-guess the intentions of God. We really need to understand the effects of usury upon the economic and social life of the community.

Any attempt to initiate thoughtful dialogue on the subject of usury is almost invariably met with defensive reactions from anyone who has a savings account, annuity, government or corporate bond, or other interest-bearing investment - which includes just about all of us.

This is understandable in view of the fact that such investments usually represent the accumulated hard-earned savings of honest people, which have been put aside for the proverbial "rainy day". Add to this the fact of chronic inflation which continually eats away at the purchasing power of such financial investments and it is no wonder that there is an army of "savers" ready to defend to the death their right to collect interest on their savings.

That is how insidious the problem has become. Most people are bewildered by the subject of economics in general, and money in particular, and see no choice but to trust the "experts". Let us begin to dispel the confusion by examining the distinction between usury and interest.

The Latin words from which these English words are derived are "usura" and "interisse". Here is how the matter is explained by Sidney Homer in his book *A History of Interest Rates* (Rutgers Univ. Press, 1963):

> "The Latin noun "usura" means the "use" of anything, in this case, the use of borrowed capital; hence usury was the price paid for the use of money. The Latin verb "intereo" means "to be lost"; a substantive form "interisse" developed into the modern term "interest". Interest was not profit but loss. "It was from exceptions to the canon law against usury that the

> medieval theory of interest slowly developed. Compensation for loans was not licit if it was a gain to the lender, but became licit if the compensation was not a net gain but reimbursement for loss or expense. The doctrine of intention was overriding."

So we see that the ideas of gain and loss were of central importance in assessing the legality of a particular contract. It was to be expected that lenders would attempt to justify all charges by labeling them "interest", and over time the meanings of the terms "usury" and "interest" became confused.

The Usury Trap

The barb in the debt hook, the thing that makes it so difficult to get free once hooked, is usury. The compounding effect of interest (usury) requires only the passage of time (and the "gracious" extension of due dates by the lender) for borrowers to sink deeper and deeper into the quicksand of debt. The obfuscation of the distinction between "usury" and "interest" has been an important factor in the evolution of the present dysfunctional and inequitable monetary system.

What the bankers call "interest" cannot be justified as compensation for loss. Neither can it be justified as compensation for services rendered, since their costs in creating money/credit are slight in comparison to the rates charged. If not for their legalized monopoly, the banking cartel would not be able to sustain such high rates and competition would reduce bank profits to a reasonable fee for services.

Debt-Money

The present global monetary system has institutionalized usury and put the money issuing power into the hands of a small banking elite. Money, in most countries, is based on nothing of real value; it is what is known as "fiat" money. The central banks limit the amount of money (actually credit) in circulation and manipulate the interest rates which are charged for "borrowing" it. It is a ludicrous but sad fact that the creation of the medium of exchange (the issuance of money) requires the people to go into debt to the banks. Those who benefit from the status quo are unwilling to acknowledge that the problem is structural; they will discuss only changes in policy (how to operate the system), avoiding any suggestion that the system might be inherently unfair, unstable, unsound and in need of revision or reform.

The Business Cycle Explained

In the present monetary system, most of the money consists of bank credit; a small percentage is in the form of circulating notes, i.e. paper bills. Money is created when a bank authorizes a loan and is extinguished when the loan is repaid. Since the amount of money in circulation is controlled by the Federal Reserve Board, and since the banks lend it into circulation and demand usury on every dollar of it, the money supply must be continually expanded to allow the usury to be paid. If the money supply is not expanded enough to offset the rate of usury, it forces default by some borrowers since there is not sufficient medium of exchange in circulation to provide all borrowers with the means to pay. This medium of exchange, which the loan contract stipulates as the form of payment, cannot be grown on farms, it cannot be dug out of the ground, nor can it be produced in shops or factories. It cannot be produced by individuals, no matter how diligent their efforts or how great their skills. It can only be created by the Federal Reserve System and the banks, which have been given the "legal" monopoly over the creation of money.

Basically, the Business Cycle arises from what I call "the something-for nothing syndrome", which in its most insidious form manifests as usury. Now the practice of usury has been institutionalized and become the very foundation of our monetary system. When money is kept in short supply and all of it is "loaned out" at interest, an imbalance is created. Where does the money come from with which to pay the interest? In order to keep the money supply from shrinking over time as interest and principal payments are made, more money must be created and more loans made. If the money supply is not expanded at a rate equal to the interest rate, some borrowers must of necessity default on their loans; the result is bankruptcies, foreclosures, unemployment, and depression.

Money growth vs real growth

When a tight money policy is being advanced by the FED it causes many debtors to default on their loans. The subsequent consequences are foreclosure by the banks and seizure of any property which has been pledged as collateral. On the other hand, if the System does allow the money supply to increase by the amount of usury required, inflation will usually result. This occurs because the growth in production of real goods and services in the economy does not normally match the yearly usury rate. If economic output is growing at a rate of say 3 percent per annum, any rate of interest greater than this charged by the banking system will result in inflation. If the average usury rate is 12% per annum, and the money supply is expanded by this amount, the aggregate production must also grow by this same percentage or more. If it doesn't, the dilution of the currency will manifest as a general increase in prices. Even if the rate of economic growth were to match the average usury rate, the productive worker would see no benefit from his increased productivity since the monetary means of its acquisition would have been accrued to the bankers in the form of interest payments. It is unreasonable to expect the natural economy to expand at the rates of usury demanded in the present system and to be driven by the artificially imposed mathematical rigor of the compound interest formula. Further, it provides that the total growth which does occur will accrue to the well-placed and privileged few but leave the majority worse off than before.

Since almost the entire money supply consists of currency or bank credit which has been borrowed into existence (and upon which the banks collect interest continuously), it is impossible for the people, in the aggregate, to ever get out of debt, for to do so under the usury system would require the payment back to the banks of more money than there ever is in existence, and would furthermore, leave the economy without any medium of exchange. The result is a virtual economic serfdom in which debtors, struggling to avoid default, are forced into an unhealthy competition with one another. It is a situation which is very much like the game of "Musical Chairs", but in this case it is far from a harmless game.

Dysfunctions of the Debt-Money System

The usury/debt-money system creates several dysfunctions and difficulties. First, it is an engine which forces inappropriate growth. The global ecological crisis is primarily the result of the debt-money system. The fact that the money, which is created out of thin air, bears an interest burden, applies pressure to the global economy to grow at a rate equivalent to the interest rate. More and more real wealth must be created upon which to base the necessary expansion of the money supply.

As shown earlier, the compound interest formula is an exponential function. That means that a debt bearing interest will grow at an accelerating rate over time. If one of your ancestors, instead of investing one hundred dollars at the founding of our country 200 years ago, had borrowed that same amount at the rate of 10 percent per year, you, his descendants would owe a debt of almost 19 billion dollars today.

Nature just doesn't work that way. Until recently, population growth and industrialization have allowed sufficient economic expansion to mask the worst effects of this absurd financial structure. Also, competitive conditions prevented interest rates from being raised to the extremes we have today. Now the limits of population growth and industrialization have been reached and the problems are becoming acute. Competitive restraints on central banks have all but been eliminated and the ownership of real wealth worldwide is ever more rapidly being concentrated into fewer and fewer hands.

Secondly, the system contaminates the social climate by (1) forcing people to devote excessive energy to the production of superfluous goods, distracting their energies from spiritual and cultural fulfillment, even while leaving vast numbers of people on the verge of starvation, (2) concentrating wealth in the hands of those who have money or control money, rather than allowing talent and industriousness to reap its proper reward, and (3) making failure inevitable for some and bringing people into conflict with one another.

Thirdly, the arrangement between governments and central banks allows governments to spend virtually as much as they wish without having to answer to their citizenry. They do this by deficit spending and inflation of the currency. If they were to be deprived of this power, the ability of states to wage war would be vastly curtailed.

It is a curious fact that in recent decades the monetary system has not been more of a popular political issue than it has. Actually, it is not so hard to understand once one sees that those who operate the system have found an ingenious way to mask its basic flaws. That strategy basically consists of using the government as "borrower of last resort" to put money into circulation. This is the only thing that has kept the system from collapse. This is quite evident from the Depression of the thirties which was an acute symptom. Keynesian economics and government deficit spending did not cure the disease, they just made it easier to live with - for a time. Now time is running out; a real cure must be found. Alternatives to the debt-money system must be developed and implemented if peace and freedom are to be preserved.

Credit restriction follows credit expansion

It is almost certain that the next few years will bring economic convulsions similar to those experienced during the 1930s. We have already had our stock market crash of October 19, 1987. If history repeats itself, a "depression" will soon follow. Following the stock market crash of 1929, the economy experienced both a shrinkage in the money supply and a reduction in its velocity of circulation. These events were not accidental but followed from a combination of monetary policies and quite predictable economic behavior.

Given the fact that the present monetary system is based on debt, the money supply must expand and contract in accordance with expansion and contraction in the amount of outstanding debt. During the expansionary phase of the business cycle, debt and money are both expanded. It typically begins with an easing of credit conditions by the banks. Making it easier to borrow on relatively favorable terms (low interest), the banks are able to induce some of those in need of capital to borrow. This puts some new money into circulation, which then gets spent on goods and services required to satisfy the pent-up demand from the previous phase of the cycle. When business seems to be expanding, other companies see the possibility for expansion of sales and profits. They too may be induced to borrow, thinking that their new profits will exceed their interest costs. There is little concern about their ability to repay loans. The monetary expansion is the result of both a willingness by the banks to lend and an inclination by individuals and organizations to borrow.

When there is a lot of money in circulation and people are spending freely (velocity is high), business is expanded. At some point, as human and capital resources approach full utilization and more money is siphoned off as profit and interest, costs begin to rise. At the same time, the available collateral becomes "loaned up" and increasing amounts of interest and principle come due. With increasing rates of inflation, the banks raise interest rates and begin to tighten up on credit. Business begins to fall off. As money begins to become increasingly scarce, there is a tendency to hold onto it. Debtors must turn it over to the banks as fast as they get it to stave off bankruptcy and foreclosure. A dollar paid against a debt disappears from circulation. The money supply tends to shrink because debts are being repaid faster than new debts are being incurred.

It is interesting to note that, in the aftermath of the 1987 market crash, the Federal Reserve System authorities, in response to federal government urgings, expressed their commitment to "provide liquidity". In simple terms this meant that the banking system was ready and willing to lend new money into circulation to prevent a chain-reaction of defaults and the kind of deflation which occurred in the 1930s. It seems that there is a general understanding today that the Great Depression was "caused" by the policies of the central bank which provided an inadequate money supply. But that is not enough to assure that the central bank will not again do the same thing. Further, as we have seen, the money supply is dependent upon not only the willingness of banks to lend, but also upon the willingness of potential borrowers to incur new debt. When the economic signs are unfavorable, individuals and businesses, seeing profit opportunities reduced and money difficult to come by, are unwilling to risk going deeper into debt. Their real wealth is declining in (monetary) value and any assets which are not already encumbered by debt are not likely to be risked by assigning them as collateral on new loans. Most everyone tries to avoid debt and maintain liquidity. Money, like any commodity when it is scarce, tends to be hoarded. The willingness of banks to lend, therefore, is no guarantee that deflation can be avoided. Maintenance and expansion of the money supply within the "debt-money" system requires, in addition, willing borrowers.

Government, Borrower of Last Resort

The greatest factor in keeping the monetary and financial systems viable over the past 50 years has been the role of the Federal Government as borrower. But this has only been the last desperate attempt to keep a flawed system from total collapse. It is widely held that the Great Depression was ended by the institution of the Keynesian prescription of "pump priming", or short-term deficit spending. But this is not an accurate account of what actually happened. In reality, it can now be seen that the government did not "prime" the pump, it provided a source of money. Government became the "borrower of last resort". When others refused to borrow or were refused credit by the banks, the Federal Government borrowed money into circulation. This began with the institution of the New Deal programs by which the Government began to borrow money and then spent it into circulation. These amounts, however, were relatively modest. It took World War II to provide an excuse for the really huge deficits required to pump up the money supply to adequate levels. The subsequent cold-war and "red herring" threat of the "Communist menace" has kept the game going.

Total public and private debt in the U. S. has grown at an average annual rate of 6.3% between 1922 and 1984. This is shown in Figure 4, which also shows the debt of the Federal government in relation to a 6.3% constant growth line projected from the 1922 level of $140.2 billion. It will be noted that Federal government debt began falling off shortly after the end of World War I but total debt, because of high levels of private borrowing, kept pace with the 6.3% growth line up until 1929. Beginning in 1931, Federal government debt began to increase again but it did not cross the 6.3% growth line until 1942. From that time on, total debt maintained its steady growth rate of about 6.3% until around 1968. From that time to the present, the rate of growth in both Federal government debt and total debt has accelerated to over 10% per year. This is a reflection of the higher "interest" rates which the monetary authorities have been purposefully maintaining. Table B shows that if the total debt continues to rise at this rate it will exceed $39 trillion by the end of the century, a figure almost 5 times the 1984 level.

No Balanced Budget

At the beginning of the Keynesian era, few people realized the true nature of the Government's role, and that once begun there would be no escape from the "whirlpool" of increasing indebtedness. Present attempts to balance the budget are not to be taken seriously. It will take more than a balanced budget amendment or Gramm-Rudman law to solve the problem. As long as money is based on debt, there can be no balanced budget without

Figure 4.

Total Public and Private Debt 1916-1984 (Top line)

Federal Gov't Debt (U.S.) 1916-1985 (Bottom line)

Compared with 6.3% annual growth line projected from 1922 (straight lines)

(logarithmic scale)

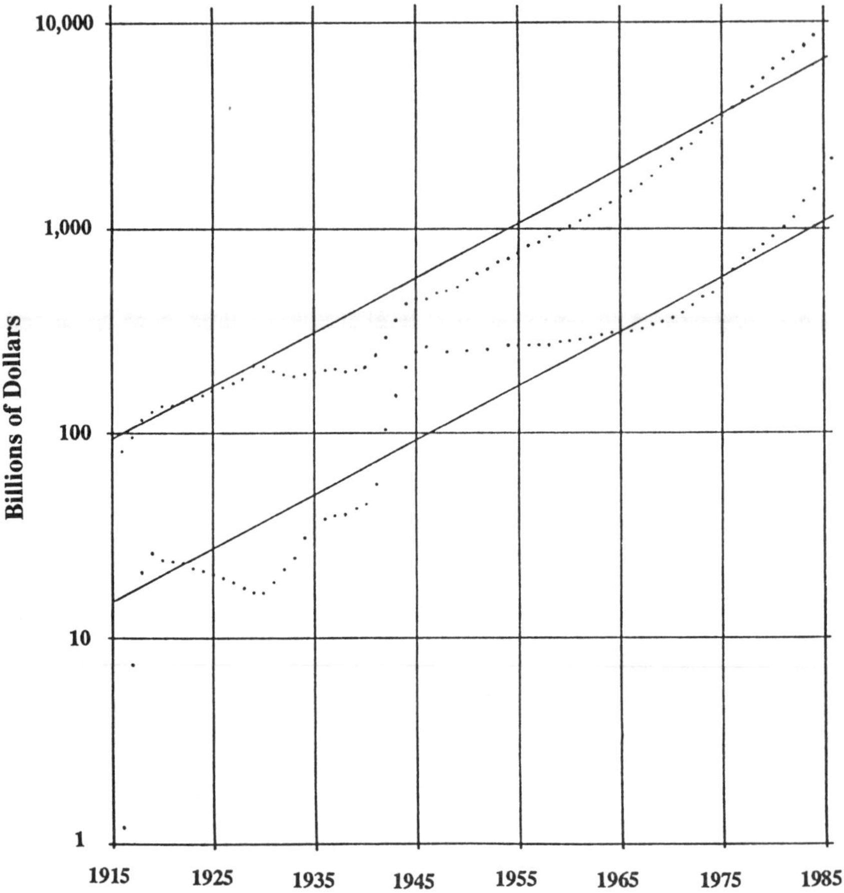

Table B

TOTAL PUBLIC AND PRIVATE DEBT OF U.S.A. - Projected 1977 to 2000

YEAR	TOTAL DEBT IN BILLIONS OF $		
	Blain method[1]	@ 6.68% [2]	@ 10.23%[3]
1976	3800(actual)		
1977	4179	4054	4188
1978	4699	4324	4617
1979	5289	4613	5089
1980	5908	4921	5610
1981	6578	5250	6184
1982	7197	5601	6816
1983	7684	5975	7514
1984	8576	6374	8282
1985			9130
1986			10063
1987			11093
1988			12228
1989			13479
1990			14858
1991			16377
1992			18053
1993			19900
1994			21935
1995			24179
1996			26653
1997			29380
1998			32385
1999			35698
2000			39350

(1) See Blain, Robert, "U. S. Public & Private Debt: 1791 to 2000"

(2) Average annual rate of debt growth, 1950 TO 1968: 6.68%

(3) Average annual rate of debt growth, 1968 TO 1984: 10.23%

wrecking the economy. Attempts by the Federal government to abdicate its role as "borrower of last resort" will bring about a liquidity crisis of unprecedented proportions. I believe that more and more people are waking up to the real nature of the game and are refusing to be caught in the debt/usury trap. If government doesn't borrow money into circulation, who will? The prospect for the future is ever increasing budget deficits and a growing national debt, bringing about an ever increasing interest expense (which amounts to a redistribution of wealth from the poor to the rich), and higher taxes to pay the interest.

What Next?

How long can this go on? Who can say? The stock market crash of October 1987 is probably an early warning sign of financial collapse, but collapse is not the worst-case scenario. Additional time may be bought at the cost of an increasingly restrictive legal climate and the further concentration of power. Interestingly, the power of the FED has continued to grow. The "Monetary Control Act" of 1980 was a huge step which virtually completes the long march toward economic totalitarianism. This Act (1) brought all depository institutions under the control of the Federal Reserve System, and (2) expanded the definition of collateral held by member banks, allowing them to purchase (and monetize) government-backed mortgages (VA and FHA), corporate bonds, and the obligations of states, counties, municipalities, and foreign governments. (CRC Bulletin #287, May 1986).

These measures can keep the system afloat by forcing the people to bear the burden of uncollectible debts, either directly through government guarantees and foreclosure and seizure of collateral, or indirectly through currency inflation. The prospect is for further expatriation of industry from the First World nations to the less restrictive climate of the less developed countries (LDCs), with their cheap non-unionized labor and lack of restrictions on environmental pollution and destruction. The fact of this centrally controlled global economy will become increasingly manifest in the political sphere with the further elimination of national distinctions, the suppression of ethnic diversity and the obliteration of laws and practices designed to maintain the integrity of national and local economies. World federation is now a reality in the economic and financial realm. Even the Communist bloc has recently joined the union. The Cold War is over and the Iron Curtain has crumbled. The political reality is that we appear to be headed, not toward a democratic world federation of self-governing nations and communities but toward a global mass society ruled by a financial elite.

At some point, most of the Third-World debt must be recognized as being uncollectible and written-off of the banks' books. When domestic austerity has been pushed upon them to the limit of popular tolerance, and there can be no further sacrifice of domestic consumption in favor of expanded exports, the debtor nations will be offered other terms. At that point, the banks will probably take direct control of their public lands and natural resources. The current vogue of "debt for nature" swaps should be given close scrutiny. It is quite likely that these measures will further concentrate land ownership and lead to the eventual despoliation of areas which they purport to protect. The money monopoly and land monopoly reinforce one another and indeed are aspects of the same problem.

How Secure Is Social Security?

Another interesting sidelight to this matter of disposal of the debt came to my attention recently when I received the June 10, 1988 newsletter from Senator Moynihan of New York. Senator Moynihan, in this newsletter, was, in all sincerity, I'm sure, patting himself on the back for his role in a "conspiracy" to, in his words, "put the Federal budget back in the black, pay off the privately-held government debt, jump start the savings rate, and guarantee the Social Security Trust Funds for a half century and more".

Now, why do you suppose, they would want to pay off the privately held debt? As of 1985, the latest year for which complete figures are available, only 17.4% of the debt was held by U. S. government agencies and trust funds, another 9.7% was held by Federal Reserve Banks, the remaining 72.9% was held by "private" investors which breaks down as follows: 20.2% held by banks, insurance companies, money market funds and other companies, 10.8% by state and local governments, 8.6% by individuals, 11.6% by foreign and international holders and 21.7% by "other miscellaneous investors".

In brief, the plan, which began to be implemented in early 1983, is to use the huge amounts of money collected from the Social Security tax to buy U. S. government bonds. Senator Moynihan's "good news" is that the budget deficits will be reduced to zero by 1993 and that the revenues from Social Security will be sufficient to retire the privately held debt by the year 2010. "It is entirely feasible", he says, "that, at that point the whole of the national debt will be owned by the Social Security Trust Funds".

I'm sure he meant that to reassure us but to me it does quite the opposite. As the Senator himself acknowledges, "you can't eat Treasury bonds". Indeed, the bonds can only be paid off out of then current tax revenues. Even if it were possible to reduce the budget deficits to zero and begin using the Social Security revenues to retire the privately held bonds, it would simply leave the then retirees holding the empty bag of uncollectible debt. What has been accomplished by this measure is the appearance that the budget deficits are being reigned in. The deficits now being reported are net after the social security surplus. Thus, the government has reported a deficit for 1987 of $150 Billion. In actuality, the deficit was $170 Billion. Fortunately, this ploy has been exposed. Estimates for 1988 and subsequent years have been provided by the Congressional Budget Office and are shown in Table C. (Reported in the Rochester Democrat & Chronicle, Sept. 19, 1988).

The Role of War

Wars provide an excuse for governments to borrow money (credit) into existence. New Zealander, Don Bethune captures the irony of this in his statement:

> "During wars there is no restraint on credit creation to produce destructive devices which are delivered free to the current enemy's home territory."

Furthermore, it should not be overlooked that wars provide a mechanism for destroying "free", unencumbered property and replacing it with assets encumbered by debt and therefore under the control of the financial powers who hold the mortgages. Thus, the rebuilding of the German and Japanese infrastructures, which had been destroyed in World War II, allowed the banks to gain tremendous leverage over those economies.

When I first encountered the notion of war being used as an excuse for credit expansion, I could not take it seriously. But the process must be at least partially conscious for people to say such things as "the War got us out of the Depression". Credit expansion may not be the intention, but the structure of the system makes it necessary, and war is its ultimate justification.

Money must be changed, as Don Bethune says, "from a debt-generating commodity on loan from the finance industry, to a social mechanism belonging to, and under the control of, the community...". Money must be demonopolized and depoliticized. All concentrations of power inevitably work to the detriment of society and the "community". I do believe that "power corrupts" and any government which is not based on community control and consensus process must inevitably become oppressive. There is more than ample experience to show that governments always inflate the money, either by issuing it directly or indirectly in collusion with financial powers. People can be free only if money and banking are free and under local community control.

Table C

SOCIAL SECURITY SURPLUS
AND THE
REAL BUDGET DEFICIT: 1987 - 1994

In billions of dollars

YEAR	REPORTED DEFICIT	SOC. SECURITY SURPLUS	REAL DEFICIT
1987 (actual)	150	20	170
1988 (est'd.)	155	39	194
1989 (prjctd)	148	52	199
1990 "	136	63	199
1991 "	131	74	206
1992 "	126	86	212
1993 "	121	99	220
1994 "	121	113	234

The Body Politic Begins to Stir

Already there are signs of rebellion. Citizens in this country and abroad are exerting pressure on their governments, partly through the political process, but mostly by direct action. One result is the refusal of some Third-World debtor nations to continue to make payments on their debts to Western banks. This will likely spawn more CIA engineered coups and military interventions by U.S. and allied forces.

In this country, as in others, there is a massive tax revolt underway which has gone largely unreported by the media. Its most important aspect is in the form of the free or "underground" economy, i.e. all the private transactions which are invisible to, and uncontrolled by, the state. As the free economy continues to grow, statist attempts to tax it will become increasingly repressive. It is likely that a new currency will be issued to flush out private stashes and that, eventually, an attempt will be made to institute a completely centralized, electronic cashless system.

In addition to the above, there is active discussion of the monetary system and a broad-based effort to abolish the Federal Reserve System. This too has been largely ignored by the media. Some pertinent facts are:

1. There is a national movement which is challenging the constitutionality of the Federal Reserve System and the monetary monopoly, and is seeking to make it a political issue.

2. The National Conference of State Legislatures has 4 times voiced its concern over the monetary system and has called for the states to act to challenge it.

3. The legislatures of 5 States (Arizona, Alabama, Indiana, Idaho and Utah) have passed resolutions calling for repeal of the Federal Reserve Act and 12 more are considering it. (CRC Bulletin #287, May1986).

4. During 1987, the Legislature of the State of Washington voted to hold a referendum on a proposal to have that State bring suit in U.S. Supreme Court challenging the constitutionality of the Federal Reserve System. The 1987 elections included the referendum, and while it did not pass, proponents managed to garner 36% of the vote in favor of the referendum - this with minimal resources to mount only a very modest informational campaign, and "slanted and inaccurate information" put out by the Washington (state) Bankers Assn. ("Honest Money for America", vol. 4, #4, Dec. 1987)

Other developments of probably greater importance are 1) the rediscovery of a vast body of Monetary Freedom literature, 2) the dedicated efforts of a small corps of modern theoreticians who are exploring the nature of money and alternatives for mediating the exchange process and, 3) the growing number of alternative exchange and local currency systems which are beginning to spring up in diverse places. Models are being developed and tried. The most promising approach appears to be the creation of a network of locally controlled (credit) exchanges similar in their essentials to those developed by Michael Linton. Linton's design, called LETS, for Local Employment and Trading System provides for the facilitation of exchange within a limited area or group without the imposition of interest charges, the use of legal coercion or the establishment of any privileged class. (See Linton and Greco, "The Local Employment Trading System", *Whole Earth Review*, vol. 55, Summer 1987).

Settling the International Debt Crisis

The centrally controlled global debt-money system has resulted in an explosion of debt worldwide. The central banks of the major western countries create money (credit) on the basis of indebtedness incurred by governments, businesses and individuals. By charging interest (usury) on this "indebtedness", wealth and power have been concentrated at the top of the political and financial hierarchies.

Debtors, in the aggregate, have been placed in an impossible situation. In attempting to comply with bank demands for payment, the governments of many debtor nations have imposed austerity upon their peoples by pursuing policies which favor production for the export market at the expense of domestic consumption and investment. These policies have been causing untold suffering and have brought many to the point of actual starvation. These same policies have been the cause of much of the degradation of their physical environments as well.

The present situation is not sustainable, neither morally, politically, economically nor ecologically. Social justice, world peace and the very survival of life on this planet depend upon a complete restructuring of monetary practices and financial accounts. The situation could be remedied with relatively little pain to anyone if the following measures were to be taken.

1. **First and foremost, the present "debt-money" system should be abandoned and an entirely new monetary system instituted.** It should be: (1) based on wealth production, not debt, (2) free of monopoly control and government interference, and (3) locally managed according to broad agreements as to standards of practice subject to independent audit.

2. Secondly, present bank claims ("debts") should be settled and eliminated within a relatively short span of time so that new, more equitable arrangements might prevail in the future.

In the interests of a harmonious transition from the present dysfunctional monetary system to a free and equitable monetary.system, it is proposed that the following terms be accepted by both "creditor" banks and "debtor" governments, businesses and individuals for repayment of credits previously extended by the banks:

1. The accrual of interest should immediately cease.

2. Repayment of principal to the banks should be rescheduled so that it takes only a reasonable percentage of income. In the case of less developed countries, domestic austerity should be eased and debt repayment reduced to a reasonable percentage of output so that it does not cause undue hardship for the population of the debtor country.

3. Repayment by less developed countries should be allowed to be made in-kind using whatever export products that have been established by that country over past years.

4. The price at which these commodities are credited against outstanding debt should be set at current market prices or at an average of recent historical market prices (over the past, say 5 years), whichever is higher.

5. Any "interest" which has been already paid or will be paid shall be counted as a repayment of principal and applied to reduce the outstanding loan balance.

Part II - Freedom And The Monetary Ideal

The Etherealization of Money

As Mark Kinney so astutely points out, each civilizational phase is based on some new communications medium which brings with it a totally new pattern of thought and behavior. This is the meaning inherent in Marshall McLuhan's famous statement that "the medium is the message".

Kinney cites Arnold Toynbee's contention that humankind is ever "etherealizing" its methods so as to achieve more with less effort. This means that each succeeding communications medium outperforms its predecessor by accessing greater volumes of information of greater precision to more people over greater distances with less effort.

This is clearly the case when we consider developments in communications technologies over the past few centuries, and especially, the computerized telecommunications channels which have exploded upon the scene within the past decade. Our methods have clearly been etherealized, not only in form but also in content. Information is increasingly abstract and symbolic, and the means of transmission is increasingly ephemeral (transitory, energetic; not concrete). Thus we see a progression from physical objects carrying information, to handwritten and printed documentation being physically conveyed, to electrical and magnetic pulses being transmitted by wire and radio/TV.

From each new communications medium emerge new behavioral patterns which are largely exchange interactions. Each civilizational phase requires the development of an exchange medium appropriate to its other elements. The key element which is missing in the current transformational stage of civilization is that of an exchange medium appropriate to the situation. The exchange medium with which we are all familiar, and which, indeed, seems to dominate our lives, is money.

Money has, in fact, been progressively etherealized. From precious metal coins and bullion which carried value within themselves, to token coins and paper notes which were symbolic representations redeemable for real money (precious metal coin), to fiat, non-redeemable notes, to bank credit and computer accounts. The transfer process likewise has become more ethereal, from physical exchange of valuable metal and tokens, to symbolic exchange using checks and money orders, to electronic transfers. The process, however, is not yet complete. In this current transitional stage, the exchange medium lags behind other aspects of the transformative process, causing the human struggle to be intensified and bringing civilization to the brink of disaster.

It is becoming more and more clear that the essential characteristic of money is (or has become) information. As Michael Linton has expressed it, "Money is information we use to deploy human effort". Ralph Haulk has added that "money validates knowledge". From these realizations, Kinney has postulated that there are two basic types of information, "*formulative* information, by which we can design and plan most any kind of project", and "*executive* information, which concerts the precise qualities and quantities of productive resources needed to put those plans into operation".

The difficulties we are facing in the present transitional stage stem from the situation that *formulative* information has become increasingly accessible to more and more people while *executive* information is still mostly monopolized. This impedes the vast majority of people from acting in ways which are consistent with their values and beliefs and their own best interests, and gives undue power to those who sit at the top of the financial and state hierarchies. The projects which get carried out are those which tend to maintain and consolidate the power of the hierarchies, which at the same time are wreaking havoc with the environment and causing vast amounts of human suffering.

The new media have brought the capability of efficient worldwide person-to-person communications, and as a consequence humankind now has the potential of realizing a condition of global, universal peace and prosperity. But this can only come about through the popularization of executive information and the devolution of power to the elemental social units.

The monopolization of executive information by governments and financial elites is embodied in their control over the process of issuing money. Governments are no longer dependent upon taxation for financing their operations. Through their collusive arrangements with the banking and financial cartel and their control over the exchange mechanisms, they are able to spend without limit and levy a hidden tax in the form of inflation. The personal income tax is not so much a mechanism of government finance as it is (1) a justification for collecting detailed information about each citizen, (2) a means of implementing social policy and (3) a control mechanism for regulating the rate of inflation of the currency.

Depoliticization of Money and Exchange

Those who control the present systems will argue that "money does not manage itself", and, of course, strictly speaking, they are right. But the issue is *how* money is to be managed and whether the state and coercive authority should have any reasonable role to play in it. It has become patently clear, based upon their past performance, that they should not. As Friedrich Hayek has argued:

> "To the present day, money is that part of the market order that government has most suppressed. It is also the part of the market order that silly rulers and economists have most tinkered with. ..it will not be present knowledge but discoveries by free experimentation that can show us the best solutions. .. government jealously guarded its monopoly, for purposes quite different from those for which money had been introduced."
>
> "Today money is chiefly not an effective medium of exchange but a tool of government for fleecing us and for "managing" the economy."
>
> "If governments were deprived of their power over money, private firms would quickly begin to define new monetary units and to issue liabilities denominated in terms of these units. Competition among issuers would compel them to seek to define their units in ways most useful to the public and to make them available to the public at the most attractive feasible terms." ("The Future Monetary Unit of Value", in *Money In Crisis*, Barry Siegel, ed., Pacific Institute, San Francisco, 1984. pp. 324-327)

Barter and the Role of Money

It is important to understand the distinction between barter and mediated exchange. In a barter transaction, or what E. C. Riegel calls "whole barter", two people exchange value in reciprocal fashion. For example, Mr. A might receive a pair of shoes from Mr. B who in return receives from Mr. A six chickens. If the value of the shoes is considered by both parties to be equal to the value of the chickens, then the transaction is complete. This is shown pictorially in Figure 5a.

Suppose, however, that Mr. A wants the shoes but Mr. B doesn't need any chickens. In that case there will probably be no trade. This is the problem with whole barter, each trader must have something the other wants, or at least can use for further trading with someone else. It was probably this latter realization that led to the development of money, and the reason why the first exchange media tended to be useful commodities. Such exchange media, however, do not change the nature of the transaction; it is still barter, or what has been called, "indirect barter". In an indirect barter transaction, one person accepts something which is not immediately useful to him but which has inherent value and can be traded to someone else. Precious

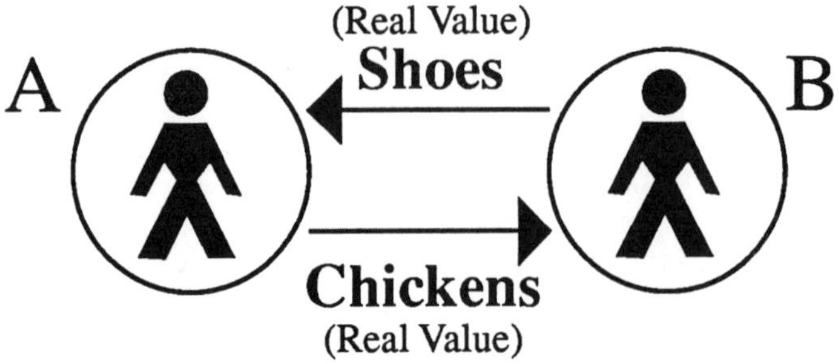

Figure 5a.

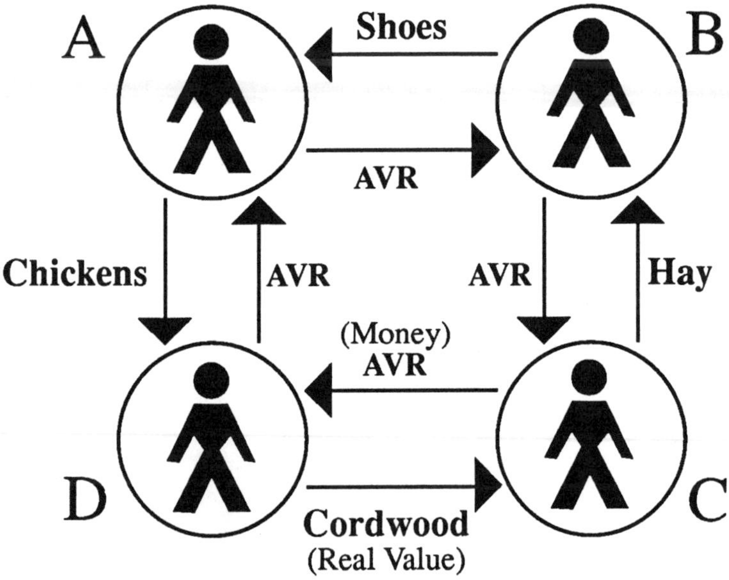

Figure 5b.

metals have historically been most commonly used for this purpose.

The inconveniences of indirect barter, in turn led to the adoption of "symbolic exchange", i.e. the use of tokens which represent items of real value, or, in other words, the transfer of claims on real value. These have taken the form of warehouse receipts, bank notes and drafts. The adoption of symbolic exchange media brought tremendous gains in convenience and efficiency. Unfortunately it also opened the door for tremendous abuses since manipulation and outright fraud became more difficult for the ordinary person to detect. Such abuses have proliferated and become the norm of official currency systems worldwide resulting in the present global monetary confusion.

It is now possible to transcend this confusion by taking the next step into an abstract monetary system. In such an ideal exchange system, all that is necessary is for traders to cooperate with one another in agreeing to accept an abstract form of payment in the form of credits issued by other traders as acknowledgment of value received. For example, suppose Mr. A buys a pair of shoes from Mr. B. He gives to B in return an "acknowledgment of value received" (AVR) or token money. B then buys some hay from C and passes on to him the AVR; C uses the AVR to buy some cordwood from D, and D in turn uses it to buy some chickens from A. Figure 5b shows this pictorially. Actually, there might be any number of trades in this circle before the AVR gets back to Mr. A. Each of the transactions in this example is called a "split-barter" because it is split into two parts with one person receiving value while the other has deferred receiving equal value to a later time and receives it from a different trader. In practice, the token can be dispensed with and replaced with an account ledger in which each transaction would result in a credit to the seller and a debit to the buyer. It is this kind of pure information medium of exchange which constitutes the ideal money.

Desiderata

The single most important feature of any potential monetary system is that the unit used to measure value be relatively invariant over time in terms of real goods and services. This is necessary mainly in order to preserve the integrity of contracts. There are essentially three reasons why an unstable monetary unit should be avoided: (1) As far as current transactions are concerned, it would appear that, if there is a general doubling of all prices, it matters not; each commodity still bears the same value in relation to other commodities, including, presumably, labor. However, confusion results when the value concept must be changed. Not all people react to changing conditions at the same pace, and some have less bargaining power than others. Labor rates typically lag behind prices of goods. Those with less accurate and timely information and those who are not so quick witted in business will suffer. (2) An even more severe problem of a changing price level is with transactions which are time dependent - claims expressed in monetary terms - debts, investment claims, insurance, etc. These presume a stable unit of measure, and fairness demands it if the intent of the contracts is to be fulfilled. It is the value of claims denominated in terms of the current value unit that can change drastically over the term of a contract. Thus, people's savings can be destroyed, totally or in part, by inflation (dilution or devaluation of the currency). Many a sad tale is to be told of investors who put their money into "safe" investments, the monetary return of which was obtained according to contract, but the purchasing power of which amounted to nil. (3) The worst of the matter is the cause - currency depreciation is due to actions which are taken by governments and banking authorities. Such actions literally rob the people of their substance resulting in economic hardship, and loss of confidence in government and diminished respect for authority.

I think that, given a choice of currencies, people will prefer to use the one(s) which maintains a stable value over time.

As Friedrich Hayek has expressed it:

> "..if people were wholly free to choose which moneys they wished to use in their daily transactions, those would do best who preferred a money with a stable purchasing power." (ibid p. 325)
>
> ..justice requires all debts to be paid in terms of units of value which the contracting parties intended, and not in what government decrees made a substitute for them. (ibid p. 334)

I think the natural tendency in an "honest" money system would be for the general price level to fall slowly reflecting technological advances and increasing productivity.

Measurement

The problems attendant to money and exchange are to a large extent derived from confusion about the nature of measurement and standards. Fairness in exchange requires accurate and precise measurement. That is why we have defined units of length, weight, volume and time, for example. We commonly use inches, pounds, gallons and hours in our agreements because they are well established and objective, and allow precise measurement. We could just as easily use hand widths, rockweights, handfuls and afternoons but these would be subjective and ill defined. We wouldn't really know what was meant or intended and equal exchange would be difficult to establish.

In order to facilitate exchange, it has become customary to use a mediating device called money. The intention of using money is to provide the seller with some evidence of the amount of value surrendered to the buyer. In measuring value, accuracy and precision are just as important as they are in measuring physical quantities such as length, weight, volume and time; indeed, value and physical quantity are inseparably linked.

In order for exchange to be fair it must be voluntary and the terms of exchange freely determined between the buyer and the seller. Further, unless it is a whole barter transaction, it is essential that there be some means of measuring value with accuracy and precision and that the unit of account remain constant over time. To better grasp the issue, let us begin with some definitions. The American Heritage Dictionary (1973), under the entry "measurement", has this to say:

> "Measurement of a quantity implies that a number is assigned to represent its magnitude. Usually, the assignment can be made by a simple comparison. The magnitude of the quantity is compared to a "standard" quantity, the magnitude of which is arbitrarily chosen to have the measure 1.
>
> There is an important distinction between a "unit of measurement" and a "standard of measurement".
>
> A *unit of measurement* is a precisely defined quantity in terms of which the magnitudes of all other quantities of the same kind can be stated.
>
> A *standard of measurement* is an *object* which, under specified conditions, serves to define, represent or record the magnitude of a unit."

Thus, in order to have a unit of account which can be agreed upon and used for fair exchange, it must be defined in terms of some standard. And what is a standard according to the above definition? It is an object. To reinforce this idea, let us further consider the established standards of physical measurement. The Dictionary continues with the following:

> "The fundamental units of the Metric System are the meter and the kilogram. The meter was defined...to be equal to 1,650,763.73 wavelengths of the orange-red radiation in vacuum of Krypton 86. The kilogram is defined as the mass of

a platinum-iridium standard, the International Prototype Kilogram, kept at the International Bureau of Weights and Measures in Sevres, France.

Now recall from the definition of measurement earlier stated that measurement involves comparison. Thus, when we measure the length of something, we compare it with a rod or tape of known length, usually one having marks showing the number of multiples of the unit which is derived from some standard. Of course, there are in practice any number of measuring devices which are constructed or calibrated using these standards as a basis. Thus we have any number of yardsticks, tape measures, scales, etc. against which comparisons may be made.

Valuing

Value itself is not an objective quantity like weight or length; it is subjective. Each person, in each situation, values each thing differently. One might go so far as to say that "value" should be used only as a verb, not as a noun. When I consider a price in the market place, I always make a comparison of that price to (1) the price of the same or similar item last week, last year, and on back in time, (2) the prices of other items which I might need or want, (3) my earning capacity per unit of time, given my range of skills, the conditions of the labor market and my present inclinations as to how I wish to spend my time and energy. Thus, my hour of labor, or more appropriately, what Don Werkheiser calls a "stress-hour", is my de facto standard. I do not think in terms of gold, nor do I care anything about gold. If the government, or someone else were to declare gold to be a "standard of value", it would not change my thinking at all, except to the extent that gold might stabilize the price level expressed in terms of the prevailing monetary unit.

The fact is that people in this country have become accustomed to valuing things in terms of "dollars". It is important to distinguish between the "dollar" we use as a value concept, and the dollar currency units provided to us by the Federal Reserve System and the government. We all have a sense of what things are worth relative to each other and over time in dollar terms. Thus, the dollar as a value concept, must be taken as given, at least for the time being. Because it is the concept we are accustomed to using, it must provide the starting point for any innovation in money and exchange.

If value is subjective and not objective, then what is it that we quantify when we speak of something being "worth" so many dollars (or francs, or pounds)? It is "price". For every transaction, a price can be recorded. The statistical compilation of prices forms the basis for stating that a certain thing is "worth" so many dollars. What we commonly take as the "value" of something is typically its "market price", however imperfect the market may be in relation to an "ideal" or "free" market. And that "market price" is actually a summary of statistical information, perhaps an average, of prices of transactions considered over a given period of time, in a given market. It is the result of the innumerable forces which influence the valuing process; the "infinite calculus of the marketplace", as Mark Kinney puts it, and it is transitory.

In sum, then, even though value is subjective and situational, it is possible to agree upon a relatively objective "standard of value" which is really a standard of prices given the existence of relatively free markets and free flow of information. We will then henceforth speak not of a "standard of value" but of a "price standard".

Standards

Efficiency in any widespread human endeavor requires the establishment of standards. Thus we have standards for the weights and measures which we use; there are standards for the recording and transmission of information (e.g. phonograph records, audio and video tapes, radio and television, etc.) and there are standards of practice in areas such as accountancy and engineering. There may be good reasons for choosing one particular standard over another, but quite often established standards seem to be quite arbitrary; the important thing is the agreement as to what the standard should be. Standards may be established by formal agreement, or they may be de facto standards derived from use and custom.

An international price standard would have obvious benefits in facilitating trade worldwide. The definition of such a standard would allow any currency, whether issued privately or by a government or central bank, to be evaluated relative to the standard and to other currencies. Adherence to such a standard would not require that issuance of currency be centrally controlled. Any issuer could maintain the value of his currency by following proper rules and procedures in its issuance. The distinction between a price standard and a currency will be taken up in detail in Part III.

Probably the best, most stable price standard would be one which derives from specified quantities of a broad assortment of basic commodities. This would be most likely to assure stability in the value of the unit of account. Thus, the "standard of value" would be defined as the price of a "market basket" containing specified amounts of specified basic commodities.

Whatever name might be chosen for the new standard accounting unit, it would be most convenient to define it to be at par with, or some round multiple or fraction of, the U.S. dollar, at the time of its creation, since that is the value concept we have established in our minds and the dollar is the closest thing there is to an international currency. The weight of history would lead us to expect that over time there would be a gradual divergence between the standard unit and official currencies as the latter continue to be inflated.

How a New Money Might Become Established

We must not be naive about the likely responses of established power to possible attempts to liberate the exchange process. As Hayek puts it:

> "...any hope for a voluntary abdication by governments of their present monopolies of the issue of circulating currency is utopian. Governments have become dependent on their power to create money for financing their own activities, since it allows them to spend in excess of the revenue they can obtain from honest taxation. They also regard their control over money as so essential a weapon of their economic policy that they will probably defend to the last not merely all the explicit powers the law has conferred, but also any others they can obtain." (op. cit. p. 330)

But there is a limit to the extent to which governments can control, either morally, legally or practically, the accounting practices and trading conventions of private enterprisers. Herein lies the key to the liberation of exchange. As Hayek puts it:

> **"The exclusive right to issue the tokens that serve as legal tender for the discharge of obligations contracted in terms of them does not preclude the use of credit accounts in other units as a general means of exchange....** The difference would be that the accounts would be denominated in terms of monetary units over which governments had no control and which, therefore, would be likely to maintain a constant value. (op. cit. p. 330) (emphasis added).
>
> ...once credit accounts in a stable unit are provided by some institutions, governments could hardly prevent the development of credit cards that, with the consent of both parties, instantly converted the amount due in a local currency into its equivalent, at the current rate, of a stable unit. Debtor and creditor would know that a certain amount of purchasing power would be due by or to them within a fixed period. Although governments would probably long resist the use within their territory of any hand-to-hand money other than

> their own, they could hardly long prevent such use of credit cards. I have little doubt that as soon as such stable private units were available, the issuers of credit cards would be well advised to use them. Indeed, I believe that it will be through the credit card rather than through any kind of circulating token money that the government monopoly of the issue of money will ultimately be broken. It is a money governments cannot confiscate when it is carried across frontiers and scarcely even when claims in terms of it are held by the recipient." (op. cit. p. 333)

Recognizing now that money is merely information, it becomes clear that a private alternative monetary unit could easily be defined at any time. All it would take is for an individual or group to publish its definition. The next step in the use of such money would simply amount to keeping accounts in terms of the new unit. This would pose little difficulty since the value of any existing currency could be converted according to the definition, just as foreign currencies are equated to one another now. Traders agreeing to keep their accounts and draw contracts in terms of the new unit could also agree to settle their accounts periodically using established legal tender money, the value of which would probably be declining over time relative to the new stable monetary unit. For this reason, they would probably eventually find some better means of settling their accounts, one which does not require them to go into the market for official currency, the value of which is beyond their control.

Ideal Money

Of all the monetary theorists of which I am aware, the one who seemed to have the greatest insights as to the real nature and function of money was E. C. Riegel. Out of these insights, Riegel conceived a "natural monetary system". Riegel refused to get entangled in the orthodox debates stating, "Only by turning our backs on the muddle of past monetary economics can we fully understand the subject of money... Error has labyrinths; truth is an obelisk" (E. C. Riegel, *Flight From Inflation: The Monetary Alternative*, The Heather Foundation, P.O. Box 48, San Pedro, CA, 1978).

Riegel's descriptions of (ideal) money cut through the armor of orthodox obfuscation and provide the basis for a rational and honest monetary system. Most pertinent are the following:

> "...money is an accounting system."

> "...money is but a medium of evidencing barter balances."

"The pure monetary medium..will be..intrinsically valueless."

"...money springs from mutual interest and cooperative action among traders, and not from authority."

"...[the issuer] must be a personal enterpriser, i.e. one who is obliged to go into the market to bid for money."

"...it is apparent that the buyer who issued the money instrument to the seller has made a commitment to the community...Thus money is actually backed by the value surrendered by the seller and potentially backed by a value in the possession of the next seller."

Definition of (Ideal) Money

Riegel's formal definition of money is as follows:

a. Money is a receipt for value
b. Expressed in terms of a value unit, and is
c. A transferable claim
d. For an equivalent value
e. To be determined by competitive exchange
f. In which the issuer is an active vendor
g. Whose issue conforms to the customs of a convention of participants in the Monetary System. (ibid p. 23)

Issuance Requirements

The kind of monetary system which Riegel envisioned can be described as a "mutual credit" or "community credit" monetary system, since the money, which is basically an I.O.U., is backed by all participants in the exchange system but identified with no particular issuer. It satisfies the conditions which I see as necessary for an honest and equitable system, i.e. it should be "convivial" (open to all qualified participants) and "reciprocal" (inherently providing equality of value exchanged).

A key aspect of Riegel's system is the recognition that only producers are qualified to issue money since only they have the wherewithal to redeem it in the marketplace. Thus Riegel prescribed free competition as the requirement for equitably regulating the value of money, i.e. its price in terms of things being traded.

He recognized that maintaining the fidelity of the monetary issue requires a formally structured monetary system and authority. The authority is necessary, not to issue the money instruments, but to (1) establish the monetary unit (unit of account), (2) prescribe the issuing process and set its limits, and (3) prescribe "the implements to be used and such mutually acceptable rules as will give dependability to the unit and to the system."

Riegel did not try to spell out these details and left much to be determined by experimentation and the free play of competing monetary systems which he hoped would someday emerge. He also did not seem to consider another question which to me seems crucial to the success of an alternative monetary system, i.e. how to insulate a new system from the existing political monetary system and to distinguish the new unit of account from the official unit. I would like to consider some of these details and express my ideas on how they might be dealt with.

Unresolved Issues

I see these as the major details which need to be worked out in implementing a new convivial and reciprocal monetary system:

1. Definition of the new unit of account in such a way as to keep it distinct from other competing monetary units and to keep its price in terms of all goods and services relatively stable.

2. Establishing criteria for qualification of money issuers.

3. Establishing Credit limits.

4. Maintaining overall system integrity.

5. Qualification of money bases (kinds of purchases for which new money may be issued).

6. Clearing/settling accounts so as to keep money a pure medium of exchange and not a store of value.

Perhaps Riegel's greatest omission was his failure to recognize that, although the exchange medium itself can, and should be abstract, the unit of account must be defined in concrete terms in order for it to have any reliable meaning over time. I believe that the best approach would be to define the new accounting unit in terms of some standard quantity and assortment of basic physical commodities. This would "ground" the new unit in reality and keep it distinct from any other value units or currencies in use. Given that the commodity assortment is sufficiently broad, it would provide a "value" unit of great stability. Once defined, any currency or credit unit could be measured against this standard. A cooperative association of producers and enterprisers could agree to keep accounts in terms of the new accounting unit and formulate agreed procedures for issuance of credits which would keep member transactions separate from and uncontaminated by established monetary and banking practice.

Considering items 2, 3 and 4, Riegel points out that the primary qualification for the issuance of money is that the issuer be willing and able to deliver goods and services to the market in exchange for money which s/he previously issued by his/her purchases. Only established producers, therefore, should be allowed to issue money and their issuing limits (maximum debit balance) should be based upon their level of trading activity within the system. This by itself may not be entirely adequate in maintaining the integrity of the system. So long as there are competing systems of exchange, there is always the possibility that a participant may choose to not honor his/her commitment, opting out of the system and refusing to deliver value equivalent to that received.

There are three possible ways, which occur to me, of handling that risk. The first possibility is to use a "funded" exchange in which each participant surrenders or pledges particular assets as security against his/her commitment. The disadvantages of this option are that it would be an impediment to trade and would tend to perpetuate present individualistic and untrusting modes of operation. A second possibility, is to maintain an "insurance" pool, funded by fees levied on all transactions, to cover any possible losses. A third possibility, which is more consistent with "fraternitarian" values and avoids the need for a coercive state authority for enforcement or confiscation of wealth, is reliance upon group co-responsibility, i.e. having each participant within an affinity group bear responsibility for the debits of the others. These groups could likewise be co-responsible with other similar groups. There might be any number of levels of co-responsibility. This is essentially the idea behind Mark Kinney's "nested" system. The advantage is that of having peer support and concerned relationships at each level. (See "Frater Market Colonies" and "Guide to Barterbuying and Bartersell-ing", from Mark Kinney, 950 Martinsburg Road, Mt. Vernon, OH 43050).

Next, the bases upon which new money would be issued should be limited, at least initially, to purchases which will manifest as necessity products in the market within a relatively short period of time, say 3 or 4 months. This would include basic raw materials and the labor to produce these goods. This is necessary, I believe, to prevent depreciation of the currency, relative to the standard unit, which would probably result from the monetization of assets which are not actually being offered on the market within the near-term. As the nested system of co-responsibility is organized and the new standards become established, these limitations might be relaxed or dispensed with.

Finally, I favor the periodic and frequent clearing of trading accounts to capital or equity accounts. In either the trading account or the capital account, a positive balance represents a claim against wealth, but in the former case it is a fixed amount against current wealth and in the latter it is a share claim against future wealth.

Part III - Segregated Monetary Functions And An Objective, Global, Standard Unit Of Account

Money, a Confusion of Functions

Money is said to serve several functions: it is (1) a generally accepted "medium of exchange", (2) "a store of value", (3) a "standard of deferred payment" and, most fundamentally, (4) "a unit of account" or "measure of value" (Dunkman, Wm. E., *Money, Credit and Banking,* Random House, New York, 1970.) We think we know what we are talking about when we use the word "money", but in fact we do not. All of the orthodox definitions of money describe its supposed functions and not its essence. Further, because the term "money" is commonly applied to a diverse array of financial instruments which are created in a variety of ways, the whole subject has degenerated into a sea of confusion. It is a curious fact that the problems arising from these contradictory functions, while they have not gone completely unrecognized, have been so completely swept under the rug.

I believe that the keys to transcending the confusion, and the creation of an equitable and efficient exchange system, free from political manipulation, lie in accomplishing the following:

1. the separation of the various functions which money is supposed to serve,

2. the establishment of an international objective standard unit of account,

3. the recognition of the true nature of the ideal medium of exchange - pure information.

The Unit of Account Function

The "unit of account" or "measure of value" function has not historically been well served by any money. Fiat monies, the type common in current use, are especially unreliable measures of value because they are undefined and subject to gross manipulation by governments and central banks. It seems not to have been widely recognized that there might be a better alternative. While money might appropriately be used in the settlement of accounts, it need not, and should not be used in defining the values to be exchanged.

Confusion of the Value Unit With a Currency Unit

The most disastrous confusion is the one which arises when the medium of exchange obliterates the meaning of the value measure or unit of account. This typically derives from state (legal tender) legislation designed to compel acceptance of a central bank issued currency. The clearest explanation of this which I have seen was given by Dr. Walter Zander in 1935, as follows:

> "Whatever the monetary system of a country, it is essential that the measure of value should be clearly and unequivocally determined. Thus, where there is a gold currency, a silver currency, or an index currency, the value should be measured by gold, silver and the index respectively. This basis of measuring economic values, and therefore of any monetary system, is destroyed when in the case of gold or silver currency the notes of the bank of issue are made legal tender, for this compels everybody to accept these notes in payment regardless of their real value. **Compulsory acceptance renders it even impossible to measure the notes by the unit of value within the country. Indeed, it establishes a legal fiction on the basis of which note and unit of value are identical.** (emphasis added). For this reason, the names of the units of value - e.g., the terms dollar, mark, pound -become ambiguous in that they mean now a fixed weight of gold and then the note of a bank of issue. Accordingly, the measure of value, on the unambiguity of which everything depends, comes to have two definitions. This renders impossible any real measurement and thus the whole monetary system is falsified." (Zander, Dr. Walter "A Way Out Of The Monetary Chaos". *From The Annals of Collective Economy*, Geneva, 1936?)

The motivation which underlies every legal tender law, of course, is the attempt by governments and their central bank cohorts to escape the consequences of their irresponsible financial manipulations. Such consequences invariably involve a depreciation of the currency in the marketplace. When legal tender is imposed to prevent the devaluation of the currency relative to an objective standard and relative to goods and services generally, then prices, in terms of the legal tender unit, must rise. This is called "inflation". Without compulsory acceptance of a currency, inflation could not occur. As Zander expresses it, "This confusion is only possible when a legal equivalence has been established between the notes of this bank and the standard of value".

"Monetary Value" and "Gold Inflation"

When speaking of a single commodity standard, e.g. gold, it is important to distinguish between its "commodity value" and its "monetary value". Whether or not there can be a "gold inflation" is a subject of long debate. The matter is complicated by the fact that the demand for gold is affected by the "gold mystique", and its monetary use, especially when other currencies are failing. Another factor is the fact that the supply of gold is ever increasing, since very little gold is "consumed", and that which is used for non-monetary purposes is largely recycled. I have come to hold the following view.

I am in general agreement with Zander, however, I would admit a "gold inflation" as a possibility, but only if gold were the sole substance of money in circulation. That is, given the use of gold as a standard of "value", a rise in the general level of prices may occur in response to a shift in the supply and demand functions for gold, but only if gold comprises the entire money stock.

When gold is used as "monetary reserves" in a fractional reserve monetary system, it is given, by agreement or decree, a price which is, in terms of other goods and services, higher than it would be if it were traded as just another commodity. This condition is possible as a result of government's power to tax, confiscate and redistribute wealth. Given that circumstance, producers will supply more gold than they would otherwise. If technology should suddenly reduce the cost of production (shifting the supply schedule), producers would be willing to supply even more gold at the official price. Government or the central bank could simply add to its "reserves" and leave prices, in general, unchanged. The inflation of the general price level does not automatically arise. On the other hand, if the monetary authority were to allow the expansion of paper money or credit based on the new reserves, inflation would result, but they need not do this. When currency was redeemable in gold on demand, inflations were relatively moderate. Redeemability placed a limit on the ability of the monetary authorities to debase the currency. Such debasement would result in increasing redemption and a loss of reserves. They would be faced with the choice of either stopping the debasement or acknowledging it with an official devaluation, i.e. an increase in the official price of gold. With the withdrawal of the redeemability feature, there exists no effective limit to official currency debasement, save the total loss of confidence in the monetary system itself.

The First Step Toward Monetary Freedom

Given the political realities of our present era, i.e. the concentration of power in state and financial hierarchies and the general lack of understanding of money and banking matters, it would be futile to attempt to gain rescission of such laws as legal tender which have become almost universal among Western nations. Any effective remedy will have to derive from private initiative. An understanding of the foregoing leads us to recommend the following prescription:

1. AN OBJECTIVE PRICE STANDARD AND UNIT OF ACCOUNT MUST BE DEFINED AND PUBLISHED BY SOME PRIVATE GROUP.

2. THIS UNIT SHOULD BE GIVEN A NEW NAME WHICH MUST BE KEPT DISTINCT FROM THAT OF ANY EXISTING OR PROSPECTIVE CURRENCY UNIT.

This unit would be used only for the accounting of values and the specification of contractual obligations. The settlement of debts would be made using any mutually agreeable currency or clearing procedure. The implementation of this prescription would allow traders to accurately account for values and to transact business more fairly and with less risk.

Criteria for Selection of a Price Standard

The confusion and inequity which arise from using an unstable official monetary unit as the unit of account cry out for an alternative. Almost any alternative measure of value would be an improvement over this situation. One of the greatest obstacles to peaceful human relations is lack of an invariant unit of account. Many proposals have been made but the question remains, - what is the most appropriate standard upon which to base a unit of account?

I think it necessary to establish some criteria to be applied in making that choice. I suggest the following:

1. The price of the standard, in terms of the totality of goods and services being traded, should be highly stable over time.

2. The standard should be relatively immune from manipulation or control by any individual or group.

3. The definition of the standard should be as simple as possible.

4. The computation of values of all products and exchange media, in terms of the standard unit, should be easily obtained.

There have been numerous suggestions for establishing a price standard. The most notable have been the following:

* some existing currency unit (e.g., dollar, mark, yen, pound)
* gold (some specified weight)
* some other single commodity (a specified weight)
* a "market basket" of commodities (composite unit)
* a unit of energy
* a unit of labor

A Single Commodity vs a Composite Standard

The question is often asked, "why is a composite standard to be preferred to a single commodity? The answer is that a single commodity is too variable in price, too easily manipulated by governments or large corporate entities and influenced too much by transitory conditions. These same objections apply to a unit of energy. On the other hand, a commodity composite would be difficult (likely impossible) to manipulate to any significant extent, and would tend to average out effects of transitory conditions on individual commodities.

Historically, perhaps the closest approach to an equitable and efficient unit of account occurred when the monetary unit was defined as a fixed weight of gold. But because gold was also used as an exchange medium, its market value in terms of other goods and services, has been distorted and tended to fluctuate. It has been distorted on the demand side by its use as money and on the supply side by the hoarding of it by both governments and individuals, especially in times of financial distress. The major disadvantages of using gold as a price standard then are (1) its price relative to all other goods and services being traded can not be expected to remain sufficiently constant over time, and (2) since objective value can only be approached by prices established in free market trade, and since gold trading is subject to extreme manipulation by governments, large producers, banks and wealthy corporations, the "objective" value inherent in a fixed quantity of gold cannot be reliably measured.

What would seem to be a far superior price standard is a fixed quantity of an assortment of specified basic commodities which are important in world trade and the satisfaction of basic human needs; what has been called a "composite unit". This idea is not entirely new, but heretofore it seems not to have been considered separately from a redeemable currency. During the 1970s Ralph Borsodi and his associates issued an experimental currency called the "Constant". The plan was to ultimately make the Constant redeemable for a "market basket" of basic commodities. While the experiment never got that far, Constants, backed by bank deposits, did successfully circulate for more than a year in parts of New England.

Borsodi had the right idea in using an assortment of commodities but his main objective was to provide an inflation-proof circulating currency. That was well and good but it made the problem more complicated and the job more difficult than it needs be. Borsodi never saw that a distinction could be made between a "standard of value" and a "basis of issue". This is clear from reading his last book, *Inflation and the Coming Keynsian Catastrophe: The Story of the Exeter Experiment With Constants* (E. F. Schumacher Society, RD 3, Box 76, Great Barrington, MA 01230, 1989). This is not at all to minimize the importance of Borsodi's work. The concepts and approach which Borsodi developed in connection with the Constant experiment, in my opinion, stand as a major advance in the development of monetary theory and practice.

I see as two separate problems the establishment of an objective standard unit of account and the creation of an inflation-proof currency. The former is primarily a matter of somewhat arbitrary definition and agreement based on statistical analysis, while the latter is a matter of proper, equitable and efficient banking practice uncontaminated by political influence or monopoly control.

Money should be purely and simply a medium of exchange. Its essence (at least in the ideal) is information, as E. C. Riegel explained in *Flight From Inflation: The Monetary Alternative*, and Michael Linton has demonstrated with his LETSystem. As such, it is valueless in and of itself. The unit of account should not be subject to wide fluctuations over time relative to the totality of prices. The price standard is analogous to a reference point in space. In space everything is in motion relative to everything else; nothing is stationary. Locations can only be stated in terms of other objects. The choice of a particular body or reference point which we agree to consider as fixed is quite arbitrary. It is the agreement which is important, though some reference points may have certain definite advantages over others.

It has been suggested that the price standard might be defined as the value (price) of a market basket of commodities as of a particular date. But fixing the date detaches us from our composite of commodities and leaves us with no means of knowing what that value was except in terms of some other unit or commodities. Any reference point must be physically identifiable at any point in time, otherwise there is no way of locating it. We cannot say, for example, that our spatial reference point is the location of the Sun on a particular date, for that point cannot subsequently be located except by reference to some other body, in which case that body would become the reference point and not the Sun. Similarly, if we want to take a commodity composite as our standard, it cannot be associated with a particular point in time.

One clear advantage of using the Sun as a celestial reference point is the fact that in its movement it takes the planets with it, leaving the planetary interrelationships unaffected. Likewise, when the value of basic commodities, as a group, changes, the value of everything else will tend to change accordingly (assuming the absence of distorting factors of privilege in the economy). Further support for this contention is found when one considers what might cause the value of commodities in general to change. This could only be the result of changes in the value of the foundational economic inputs - energy and labor, which, to some extent are interchangeable. I believe that further analysis of the relationships within this value hierarchy will clarify and strengthen the case in favor of a composite commodity price standard.

Defining the Composite

A composite standard will not have a perfectly fixed value over time, but it will be much more invariant than anything else which has ever been used, and its use in accounting and contracts will be a giant leap forward in the liberation of the exchange process. The following are my criteria, in approximate order of importance, for selection of the commodities which would define the price standard:

1. traded in several relatively free markets (free exchange).
2. importance in world trade (volume).
3. importance in satisfying basic human needs (necessity).
4. stability of prices (in real terms) over time (stability).
5. uniformity of, or standardization of quality (uniformity).

No doubt these criteria are highly correlated with one another anyway so this particular ordering probably need not be strictly adhered to. Borsodi selected 30 commodities as a basis for his "Constant" and, according to Bob Swann, one of Borsodi's close associates in the Constant experiments, the 30 proved to be as stable as larger composites (involving a greater number of commodities) which were considered. The thirty commodities which Borsodi used for his Constant currency could be taken as a starting point, each being evaluated according to the above criteria (See Appendix C). Some would likely be dropped and others added. Once a reasonably good mix is settled upon for the price standard, a unit of account, defined in terms of the standard should be published and given a unique name. Any circulating currency could then be evaluated relative to the standard and its unit using the readily available market prices prevailing at any point in time.

Expected Results

I believe that the publication of such an objective international price standard and unit of account will result in the following outcomes in quick succession:

1. Traders will quickly see the advantages of using the new unit in keeping their accounts and will begin to do so.

2. As political currencies become more unstable and international finance more chaotic, traders will begin drafting their exchange agreements in terms of the standard accounting unit.

3. New, non-political, free enterprise exchange systems and currencies, which hold their value close to par with the standard unit, will come into being and displace present national currencies.

The Effects of Legal Tender

It is legal tender laws which attempt to establish the price of a currency by decree. Such an outcome, however, is in defiance of natural law. Only in appearance can it be achieved and this is by the process of obliteration and abandonment of objective price standards. Given an objective price standard which can be kept distinct from any legal tender currency unit, government and bank manipulated currencies, if accepted at all, would be accepted only at a discount from par. No longer could the dilution of official currencies be camouflaged.

Legal tender requires that the currency be accepted in payment. It further requires that a creditor owed an amount of X dollars must accept X dollars as payment in full; that he cannot demand more than X dollars. In other words, the money must be accepted at par, regardless of how shamelessly it may have been manipulated in the interim between the incurring of the debt and its payment. But traders need not take as their reference point a constantly manipulated accounting unit such as the "dollar" but can choose an objective unit defined in terms of a fixed quantity of physical commodities, which would be impossible to manipulate.

If, then, accounts are kept in terms of some objective accounting unit (let's call it a "VAL" for the time being) rather than in dollar terms, a creditor could demand, as justice requires, an equal number of VALs in payment.

He might be willing to accept dollars but the amount of dollars would be determined by the market value (price) of dollars in terms of VALs at the time of payment, which could easily be determined from the current prices of the commodities in the market basket. Traders could thereby protect themselves against currency dilution and devaluation.

How governments would respond to the existence of an objective accounting unit is difficult to predict. They certainly would not initially give it support since it would make their irresponsibility all too apparent and tend to constrain their power. They would perhaps attempt to legislate it out of use. I have been informed by one source that it is the policy of the Internal Revenue Service to attempt to tax as a capital gain any dollar amount of increase resulting from fulfillment of an indexed contract. Thus, if a contract were written to try to assure that the same value delivered today would be repaid tomorrow, any increase in the number of dollars required, resulting from depreciation of the dollar in the interim, would be taxable. Hopefully, however, saner minds will eventually prevail in fostering use of the objective standard unit, seeing that it is essential to preventing financial chaos.

What About a Labor Standard of Value?

It has often been noted, and rightly so, that human labor is the basis of all value. Granted that the Earth is the source of our material sustenance, its bounty cannot be accessed or made usable without the application of labor. Even in simple societies which live close to nature the fruit must be gathered and the game hunted. This recognition has led some to propose that a labor hour be used as the objective standard accounting unit. But how is a unit of labor to be defined? Is it a unit of time spent in labor, and if so what kind of labor, and whose? Some workers are more skilled than others and not all labor is equivalent in value. Labor is too vague a concept for the purpose of value measurement. Bilgram and Levy, in *The Cause of Business Depressions*, state that "we can only obtain a conception of the value of labor by its fruit". In consideration of the above I have never favored the idea of establishing a labor hour as a price standard.

The motivation which I perceive in those who advocate a labor standard of value is to correct the vast and obvious inequities in the labor markets. I share those motives but the problem will not be solved by choosing a labor standard as the basis for the unit of account. One must understand that, at present, the trade arena is polluted by privilege which manifests as usury and "super-rents", which are conceptually the same thing. But the establishment of fair and free labor markets requires much more than the definition of a price standard. When I go to market, my purchase agreements are based upon the utility to me of the products offered and not upon the amount of effort which produced them. If the distortions created by privilege in the marketplace are eliminated, then the producer would be assured of a fair return for his/her labor.

Finally, it should be remembered that impersonal trade is only one type of economic exchange. It has its place but should not be expected to accomplish all of the results which are more appropriately obtained by other types of (closer) interpersonal interaction.

Power to Issue Money

At present, monetary issue is still monopolized by virtue of state granted privilege. This is what presently makes money-mediated trade a negative-sum game, and is the primary problem which must be remedied. A convivial (open to all) exchange system derives from distribution of the power to issue, which is dependent on the allowed basis of issue of a currency and not upon the choice of a price standard or unit of account. Josiah Warren and Proudhon attempted to democratize economics by "generalizing" the basis of issue; in effect, allowing workers to monetize their own labor. This was a step in the right direction.

Both businesses and individuals are increasingly learning to cooperate in creating exchange mechanisms which do not rely upon the use of official currencies or bank credit. So called "barter" exchange, or more properly "reciprocal trade" is becoming very popular among even some very large businesses. They have discovered that their trading need not be limited by an insufficiency of official currency or the willingness of banks to lend, and that they can provide their own interest-free medium of exchange in the form of credit which all agree to honor.

The same general principle is applied in Michael Linton's Local Employment and Trading System and Conrad Hopman's Community Cooperation Coordinator. Linton's LETSystems, of which there are several currently in operation, are intended to be strictly local and limited to supplementing the official currency system. Hopman's plan is more far-reaching and incorporates a wide range of agreements which comprise a quasi-legal system.

Mark Kinney, recognizing the need for restructuring of social interrelationships as well, has proposed a socio-economic reorganization with global possibilities. The unique feature of Kinney's vision is its emphasis on what I call "co-responsibility". Kinney's system, called the "GEN$ystem" (for Global Economic Net-dollar System), is similar in concept to LETS but instead of joining as individuals, members join as part of a group in which the group is responsible for each of its members. The GEN$ystem uses a "nested" structure: each individual is part of an affinity group which is part of a "Base Group"; several Base Groups comprise a "Union", several Unions comprise a "Neighborhood", these, in turn, are nested within "Self-Reliance Leagues" which are nested within "Areas", and so on, potentially up to the global level.

The idea of being co-responsible may take some getting used to, especially for Americans who tend to be individualistic and non-committal, but participation is intended to be completely voluntary and the idea should appeal to the increasing numbers of people who are being marginalized and feeling alienated within the mass society. And as Kinney puts it, the reason for nesting is "not just to be sure that everyone is honest, which is important, but to insure, by the same process, that everyone is successful." If an entire nest of any type (Base Group, SR League, or Area, etc.) develops a "poverty spiral" in its total balance of payments, "information will be accessed by their next larger nest capable of reversing that trend". (Mark Kinney, *A Flow Chart For Liberation: A Hypothesis of History And a Liberative Strategy For The 1990s*. New Civilization, 16255 Ventura Blvd. #605, Encino, CA 91436). In other words, the other groups within a nest, seeing that one of their peers is having difficulty in providing as much value as it receives, will come to its assistance with whatever information is necessary to assure its viability.

Confusion of Currency with Assets

The inappropriateness of using money as a "store of value" has also been recognized. Dr. Dunkman has stated:

> "To the extent that money is used in the asset or holding function (store of value), this money is not being used as a medium of exchange. Thus a single financial instrument is being used for two diametrically opposite functions, in the sense that, if the purpose of money is to be spent, then money is used as a medium of exchange; if the purpose of money is to to be held as an asset, the money is not to be spent. As we shall see, this duality makes the theory of money more complicated than it would be if money had but one function. ...The inclusion of the storer of value function introduces a confusion into the definition of money." (op. cit. p.15)

Rather than talk about "money", a subject which has been totally confused, let us consider the two objectives of (1) facilitating exchange and (2) storing value, and consider how each might be achieved independently. The previous section (Part II) dealt in detail with the characteristics of an ideal exchange system. All that is needed here is to describe the process of clearing balances and adjusting ownership claims. The ideal exchange system could be described as a "producer credit exchange system" or "mutual credit exchange system", in which each producer is authorized to incur a debit balance up to a certain limit based upon his past or expected volume of sales. The totality of debit or credit balances within the system would be analogous to the money supply, but in this system it would be self-adjusting since the "money" is created as needed by traders themselves.

Separation of Saving From Exchange - Value Storage

One problem which may arise in a system of exchange is stagnation within the system which can result from idle balances, either credit or debit. Those holding idle debit balances, in effect, would not be honoring their commitments in a timely manner. Those who hold idle credit balances would, in effect, not be demanding from the market value which is due them. This can be a problem because the system is intended primarily to facilitate trade. The primary problem to be overcome in facilitating trade is the "barter limitation", i.e. the fact that the buyer may not have anything the seller wants. By creating an intermediary "medium of exchange" there is a "space" created within which the seller may supply the buyer's need anyway and then proceed to find a supplier for his own need. This "space" is only partially temporal; mostly it is interpersonal, a matter of matching up specific needs or wants with appropriate supplies in the market. In other words, it allows some slack in which people can find one another so that each can have his/her needs satisfied.

Credit balances create a demand pressure upon the market, since creditors are yet to be satisfied, while debit balances create a supply pressure on the market, since debitors are committed to deliver value to the market. Idle credits mean that value supplied to the market is not being taken up as expected. A possible consequence of this is that suppliers, seeing slack demand, will reduce prices and adjust their production downward. Idle debits, on the other hand, mean that value is not being supplied to the market as expected. With supply deficient in relation to the credits seeking satisfaction, there will be a tendency for active suppliers to raise their prices and to adjust their production upward to satisfy the apparent increase in demand.

In a centrally controlled monetary system in which the supply of money (or credits) is artificially restricted, both of the above described conditions are experienced, usually in cyclical fashion and with catastrophic consequences for at least some portion of the population. In a free "mutual credit" exchange system, in which credits (and debits) arise automatically in the course of trade, the problem would presumably be much less severe, but that does not mean it can be ignored. In the design of such a system, steps should be taken to prevent its becoming problematic. What steps would be appropriate?

Before considering the answer to that question, let us focus on a second necessary function in finance, the store of value. The term "store of value" is a metaphorical phrase. Since value is an abstract concept and not a physical quantity, it cannot really be stored. Cabbages can be stored, wheat can be stored, building materials can be stored, metals can be stored, but each, of course, is subject to some degree of deterioration over time. The problem to be solved by storage is the asynchronicity of supply and demand. The very idea of storage is based on the desire to match present supplies with future needs. We put aside the extra food from the garden in summer to satisfy our hunger next winter when the garden will not be producing. Similarly, we save during our productive years so that we can have the means of livelihood during our retirement years, but unlike our storage of food from the garden, which we do directly, our saving for retirement we do socially.

Ultimately, at any point in time, non-producers are dependent upon then current producers for the satisfaction of all their needs and desires. The mechanisms by which the needs of non-producers are met are varied and often complex and are based on such factors as values, ethics, social norms, legal statutes and financial agreements. In our retirement years for example, we are mainly dependent upon two basic arrangements (1) coercive redistribution of wealth by governments in the form of such programs as Social Security and Welfare and (2) contractual agreements of a form usually called "investments" (including pensions) which consist of such financial instruments as stocks, bonds, mutual fund shares, bank deposits, etc..

In either event, what we have can be called a "claim" against current or future production. The question of which claims may or may not be "legitimate" is, of course, always open. And the question of which claims may or may not be honored is always a matter of concern. It has been suggested that, in order to make exchange credits a pure medium of exchange, the imposition of levies upon either debit or credit balances, or both, might be used. Levies applied to debit balances would constitute a form of interest, while levies imposed on credit balances have been called "demurrage". Given our conditioning and the prevailing practices within the conventional systems of money and finance, there is a greater tendency to favor the imposition of levies or charges upon debit balances rather than upon credit balances, debit balances being thought of as loans from the community to the debitor, and the levy representing an interest charge. Given what has been said above, I think it can be seen that the matter is not so "cut-and-dried". Also, different considerations apply depending on whether we are talking about short-term claims which facilitate exchange or long-term claims which represent the "storage of value".

Some have argued that, in order to keep an exchange system vital, it is more important to impose a periodic levy upon credit (positive) balances (See, for example, Silvio Gesell, *The Natural Economic Order.*) This "demurrage" would encourage the spending of credit balances, and insure the lively flow of "money" through the system. Indeed, several issues of "stamp scrip" issued during the Great Depression of the nineteen thirties used the demurrage feature. If credits are thought of as money, this seems to make sense. Likewise, if debits are thought of as debts, an "interest" charge on them also seems to make sense. But, if we can separate in our thinking the two functions of facilitating exchange on the one hand and value storage on the other, then I think it becomes clear that in a system of pure exchange, neither is necessary nor efficacious.

The imposition of levies upon either debit or credit balances, or both, as a way of promoting their use as an exchange medium is counterproductive to the main objective of "reciprocity", i.e. equal value for equal value. Since everyone benefits from the facilitating power of the system, buyers and sellers should bear an equal burden in the cost of its operation, and this burden should be kept to a minimum.

In order to prevent the use of exchange credit balances for value storage or the use of debit exchange balances for long-term financing, both could be time-limited. I would handle the matter by limiting both the amount of debits and credits which could be carried over from one period to the next. I would propose to periodically "clear" exchange balances to a capital account. Anyone who has purchased more than he/she has sold during the current period, or who wants long-term financing for any purpose, must find someone who is willing to assign his/her credits for a specified period. This is a capital market function.

Likewise, anyone who desires to "save" his/her credits, must find some suitable investment medium for accomplishing the storage of his/her value. In other words, side-by-side with the exchange system, there should exist a capital market in which savers and entrepreneurs can be brought together; in which surplus balances held by some can be allocated to others (savings or storage of value) to be used in capital formation (investment) or to finance consumer durables.

Those traders holding credit balances, which means that they have delivered more value than they have received, have a general claim against wealth owned by those holding debit balances. Similarly, those with debit balances have a commitment to deliver that much value to the community.

Rather than allow these claims or commitments to be held indefinitely, they should be "cleared" (reduced to zero) at frequent intervals. This would tend to make these balances a pure exchange medium and extenuate the store of value function. The fact that the exchange medium is readily available to all producers and may be created as needed in the course of trade will tend to make it valueless in and of itself. Also, its value will diminish further the more frequently the balances are cleared.

The next question to be answered is, "What is the nature of this 'capital account'"? If the trading balances represent claims within a "current account", and they are strictly for the purpose of facilitating exchange, then the resultant increases or decreases must be translated into changes in ownership of real wealth. Thus, each trader, in addition to having a current account, would also have a capital account representing his/her ownership share of some real assets or long-term claim against future production. These assets might be in the form of real property or capital equipment, while the claims might take the form of equity shares, e.g., common or preferred stock in productive enterprises. These instruments would constitute the store of value.

Capital formation is the creation of new businesses or the expansion of existing ones. It includes construction of buildings, improvement of land, production of tools and equipment, and other expenditures which are expected to be recovered over a long period of time.

In each case, whether current account or capital account, a credit balance represents a "claim", and the activity which gives rise to the claim should determine whether it is "currency" or "capital". In the former case it is a short-term claim upon the market which is intended only to facilitate trade. It is a "demand" deposit which the market should be able to satisfy at any time. In the latter case it is a long-term claim against assets which are not liquid, e.g. if the claim has resulted from activity which has produced tools, it will take time for the cost of the tools to be recovered in the production of consumable goods and their sale in the market.

One of the "sins" of the present banking establishment is that they have blurred this distinction between savings deposits and demand deposits. Formerly, banks paid no interest on demand deposits because, being subject to immediate withdrawal, they could not be invested in income earning assets. Properly, demand deposits represent goods (and services) presently in the market and available for purchase, while savings deposits represent investments in capital goods and durables. Now banks are paying interest on demand deposits and giving some savings deposits much the same liquidity as demand deposits.

The way in which I propose to separate the medium of exchange from the store of value is not new and it is neither cumbersome nor problematic. It is as easy as transferring deposits from your checking account to your savings account, or buying shares of stock or a mutual fund. Indeed, much of what needs to be done in solving the financial crisis is to restore sound banking practice. Since the monetary and financial authorities seem unwilling to do it, the people themselves will have to rebuild the system from the ground up, based upon the principles of equity, conviviality and reciprocity, and a clear understanding of the effects of various financial practices.

OVERALL STRATEGY for liberation of exchange and enhancement of cooperation.

To summarize my prescription for solving the monetary mess, I propose implementation of the following steps:

*Definition and declaration of a global price standard (comprised of a composite of basic commodities), and the definition of an objective unit of account based upon this standard.

*On-going monitoring of markets and prices, and computation of currency values in terms of the objective unit of account.

*Establishment of independent local exchange systems, reciprocal trade exchanges or clearing houses to provide interest-free exchange mechanisms under community control.

*Establishment of capital markets separate from the exchange systems but also under community control.

The networking of these locally controlled exchanges and their adherence to an appropriate set of principles and protocols could provide an equitable world-wide mechanism for exchange and material security for all.

Appendix A

Definition of an Objective, Global Standard Unit of Account Using a Composite (Market Basket Assortment) of Basic Commodities

Defining the Standard

The definition of a composite commodity standard can be achieved by completing the following steps:

1. Select about 30 commodities to be included in the standard, based on the following criteria:

   1. traded in several relatively free markets (free exchange).
   2. importance in world trade (volume).
   3. importance in satisfying basic human needs (necessity).
   4. stability of prices (in real terms) over time (stability).
   5. uniformity of, or standardization of quality (uniformity).

2. Determine the "economic importance" (I) of each commodity by multiplying its average price (P) during the base year in one specified market (e.g. New York) by world production (V) of that commodity in the base year. Thus

   $I = P*V$

3. Determine the fractional weight (W) for each commodity in the market basket by dividing its economic importance by the sum of all the economic importance figures. Thus

   $W = I/\text{sum } I$

4. Selecting the initial value of the market basket arbitrarily to be equal to, say, $1,000,000 (one million dollars), determine the initial value amount (D) of each commodity to be included by multiplying its weight (W) by $1,000,000. Thus

   $D = W*\$1{,}000{,}000$

5. Determine the physical quantity (Q) of each commodity to be contained in the market basket by dividing its value amount by its average price (P). Thus

Q=D/P

6. Adjust the quantities (Q), discarding fractional units in such a way as to not disturb too greatly the relative make-up of the market basket while maintaining its initial value close to $1,000,000.

7. Consider the value of the final market basket to be (arbitrarily) equal to 500,000 (five hundred thousand) standard accounting units. Thus, the standard unit will be initially equivalent to about $2 US, or $1 will equal .5 standard units.

The process described in Steps 1 through 6 above reduces to taking the same fraction of each commodity's total world production, that fraction being $1,000,000 divided by the total value of world production of all the selected commodities.

Determining the Value of Currencies in Terms of the Standard Unit.

Given the definition of the standard unit of account as being one five hundred thousandth of the specified "market basket", the value of any currency (e.g. the U.S. dollar) at any time can be easily determined by computing the current cost of the market basket in dollars using prices reported in actual trading. Dividing by 500,000 will give the dollar equivalent of one standard accounting unit. The reciprocal, of course, would be the value of the dollar expressed in standard accounting units.

Appendix B

Dialog on the Composite "Value" Unit

Bilgram and Levy, (Bilgram, Hugo & Louis Edward Levy, *The Cause of Business Depressions*, J. B. Lippincott, Philadelphia, 1914) raise a number of objections to the use of a composite unit, all of which I believe are without merit. They, like Borsodi, seem not to have made the distinction between using the composite as an accounting standard as opposed to using it as a basis of issue for a currency.

In section 31, they do mention in passing the kind of standard I am proposing. They say,

> "Some writers.....have proposed a composite or multiple unit (321), consisting of a definite number of staple articles in definite quantities. The total value of the items is to constitute a standard sum, such as one hundred or one thousand dollars, according to the composition of the list. Of course, by this expedient only an approach to an idealistic unit could be obtained".

Well, what's wrong with that? If an ideal standard is impossible, then we must find the closest possible approach to it. However, it should be given a name different from any existing currency or any prospective currency. In section 32, they seem to favor a gold standard, saying, "While the gold denominator is not altogether free from objection, no available substitute appears to be preferable". I disagree. I think it is indisputable, based on the historical evidence, that a composite standard would be much more stable than a fixed weight of gold or of any other single commodity. Their arguments against a composite commodity standard seem specious to me. Let us consider these in turn.

1. It is true that "most goods are produced in different grades of quality" but the commodity markets seem to have no trouble in dealing with this. They do not seem to be plagued with "frequent disputes as to proper quality". This is not a significant objection.

2. Their next objection expresses a multitude of confusions and non-sequiturs. It does not matter that "each commodity will vary in price". Some will rise relative to the others and some will fall, but the value of the composite should remain fairly constant relative to all other goods and services being traded. They say, "there is no economic force by which the market value of things generally can become related to a prescribed unit of

this kind". Well, I say, if each commodity which makes up the composite is freely traded, then the value of the composite is established in terms of any single commodity or any currency. The composite itself need not be traded as a "market basket". We are agreeing by definition on a new accounting unit, the value of all currencies, goods and services to be measured in relation to it and not the other way around.

3. Their last objection is "the difficulty of making the value of money conform to a given composite unit". I grant that this would be difficult, but happily, it it not at all necessary. What we are looking for is something which would serve as a determinate unit of account and preserve the integrity of contracts, and against which the value of any currency could be measured. The use of such a unit would clearly show up any currency dilution which heretofore has manifested as general price inflation in the marketplace. Instead of currency dilution forcing prices up, it would force the price of the currency (in terms of the standard unit) down. In other words, traders would discount the currency.

Bilgram and Levy's book is a masterful work on the subject of money, but one must keep in mind the times in which it was written and the mindsets which were predominant then. They too seem to have had their biases and blind spots. This is clearly evidenced in section 321 where they state:

> "While a number of contributory causes have been at work to raise the cost of living, the principal cause is no doubt to be found in the vast improvements made in the metallurgy of gold. Through the introduction of the cyanide process gold is now obtained with less labor and cost than formerly".

Well, clearly that argument no longer applies, if it ever did, since current money has no relationship to gold. Further, I think a careful study of history shows that price inflations in terms of gold-backed currencies have occurred many times. And to the extent that the statement is true, it simply supports my argument against the use of a single commodity as the defined reference point for measuring values.

In the last paragraph of that section they take another poke at their "straw man", the volume theory of money, where they allude to the impossibility of controlling the value of the currency through manipulation of its volume in circulation. But there is nothing to be gained by being drawn into this debate. They say nothing about how the currency is put into circulation, and this is the crucial question which determines its value. The process of official currency dilution is analogous to the farmer pumping water into his milk. The total volume of fluid is increased but that is not the significant factor. What is significant is the fact that a given volume of fluid now contains a lesser amount of nutritional value. Similarly, the addition of false (albeit, legal) claims to the real claims within the money stream (dilution of currency) results in a lower value content in each currency unit.

Bilgram and Levy seem to have been unable to separate the ideas of "standard of value" and "medium of exchange". In section 111 they show that they are hung-up on redeemability. They object to a composite standard on the grounds that the currency would have to be redeemable in the market basket of commodities. If a currency is properly issued, however, on the basis of the production of real value, its value should remain at or close to par with the standard unit without redeemability. A properly issued currency will always be redeemable in the marketplace. Under monetary freedom, traders will choose to use those currencies which show themselves to be most stable in terms of their purchasing power.

After all their objections, B & L grudgingly concede in paragraph 4 that an "index number" based on a composite of commodities would allow the mean price level of all things to be kept approximately stable, and they mention Irving Fisher's work in this regard. They question the workability of it in practice but offer little in the way of specific support for that argument. They perhaps did not fully comprehend index numbers which were then quite a new concept. They may, however, have had just cause to question the workability of such an approach given the state of development of markets, transportation and communications systems of their day (1914) and the lack of computing equipment. Conditions are much different today and index numbers of various kinds have been in common use for some time. I think there is little question now that such an approach is practical.

Appendix C

Note on Ralph Borsodi's "Constant" Currency

In 1972, Ralph Borsodi and a few associates set-up an organization called Independent Arbitrage International with the object of conducting some experiments in privately issued money. They set out to prove two things, (1) that "an honest private money could be circulated with a fair degree of public acceptance and without automatically facing interference by the government", and (2) "that a form of paper money could be issued that would neither inflate nor deflate".

Borsodi's strategy for making his currency inflation-proof was to make it redeemable. The Constant was to be redeemable for a "market basket" of "the world's 30 major raw material commodities". The unit of repayment for the Constant was defined as follows, with the total "market basket" being equivalent to fifty thousand (50,000) Constants:

Gold, 60 Troy ounces	Aluminum, 500 lbs.
Petroleum, 400 Barrels	Sugar, 6,000 lbs.
Iron, 15 Short tons	Rubber, 500 lbs.
Rice, 20,000 lbs.	Soy Beans, 50 Bushels
Wheat, 400 Bushels	Oats, 100 Bushels
Silver, 40 Troy oz.	Cotton Seed, 1 Short ton
Corn, 350 Bushels	Rye, 50 Bushels
Cement, 125 Barrels	Hides, 10 Pieces
Cotton, 2 Bales	Zinc, 300 lbs.
Wool, 250 lbs.	Lead, 200 lbs.
Cocoa, 1,500 lbs.	Jute, 200 lbs.
Barley, 200 Bushels	Tin, 20 lbs.
Peanuts, 1,000 lbs.	Nickel, 30 lbs.
Copper, 500 lbs.	Sulphur, 1 Long ton
Coffee, 3 Bags	Copra, 1 Short ton

A facsimile of a 25 Constant note is shown on the following pages.

Dr. Borsodi's objectives were only partially achieved. In a report which appeared in the Fall, 1975 issue of *Green Revolution*, *(p. 7)* Borsodi, then age 89, had this to say:

> "I personally conducted the Exeter Experiment for over a year during '72-'73 to show the feasibility of circulating privately issued money, both in the form of paper currency and in the

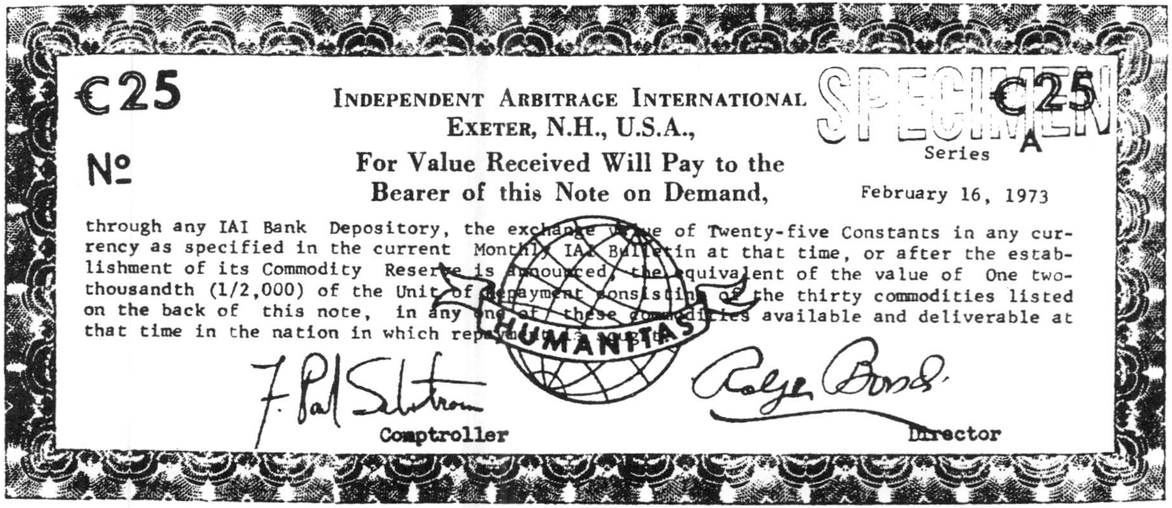
€25
INDEPENDENT ARBITRAGE INTERNATIONAL
EXETER, N.H., U.S.A.,
SPECIMEN
€25
A
Series
№
For Value Received Will Pay to the
Bearer of this Note on Demand,
February 16, 1973
through any IAI Bank Depository, the exchange value of Twenty-five Constants in any currency as specified in the current Monthly IAI Bulletin at that time, or after the establishment of its Commodity Reserve is announced, the equivalent of the value of One two-thousandth (1/2,000) of the Unit of Repayment consisting of the thirty commodities listed on the back of this note, in any one of these commodities available and deliverable at that time in the nation in which repayment is sought.
HUMANITAS
Comptroller
Director

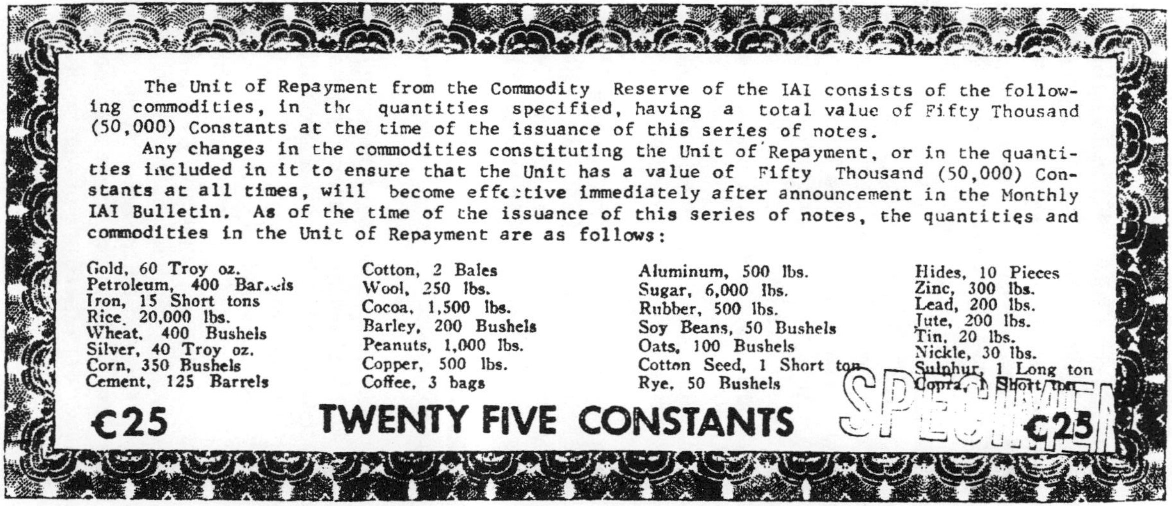

The Unit of Repayment from the Commodity Reserve of the IAI consists of the following commodities, in the quantities specified, having a total value of Fifty Thousand (50,000) Constants at the time of the issuance of this series of notes.

Any changes in the commodities constituting the Unit of Repayment, or in the quantities included in it to ensure that the Unit has a value of Fifty Thousand (50,000) Constants at all times, will become effective immediately after announcement in the Monthly IAI Bulletin. As of the time of the issuance of this series of notes, the quantities and commodities in the Unit of Repayment are as follows:

Gold, 60 Troy oz.	Cotton, 2 Bales	Aluminum, 500 lbs.	Hides, 10 Pieces
Petroleum, 400 Barrels	Wool, 250 lbs.	Sugar, 6,000 lbs.	Zinc, 300 lbs.
Iron, 15 Short tons	Cocoa, 1,500 lbs.	Rubber, 500 lbs.	Lead, 200 lbs.
Rice, 20,000 lbs.	Barley, 200 Bushels	Soy Beans, 50 Bushels	Jute, 200 lbs.
Wheat, 400 Bushels	Peanuts, 1,000 lbs.	Oats, 100 Bushels	Tin, 20 lbs.
Silver, 40 Troy oz.	Copper, 500 lbs.	Cotton Seed, 1 Short ton	Nickle, 30 lbs.
Corn, 350 Bushels	Coffee, 3 bags	Rye, 50 Bushels	Sulphur, 1 Long ton
Cement, 125 Barrels			Copra, 1 Short ton

€25 TWENTY FIVE CONSTANTS SPECIMEN €25

form of hundreds of checking accounts at five different banks. Toward the end of the experiment, the equivalent in Constants of $160,000 was in circulation. This, to my satisfaction, proved that an honest private money could be circulated with a fair degree of public acceptance and without automatically facing interference by the government. Unfortunately, the Exeter Experiment was only a partial test of the Constant Currency system - the public part. The part of the system that would provide the commodity backing was not set up. Many people misunderstood this. If the complete Constant Currency system had been in operation, there would have been no reason to end the experiment, since it was a success as far as it went. I proved what I'd set out to prove. Now it's up to some younger people to carry on and set up a complete Constant Currency system. The International Monetary Fund has recently decided to eliminate the use of gold, completely now, in international transactions. -Just as President Nixon has ended all relation between gold and the U.S. dollar. The monetary system of the non-Communist world is based on the U.S. dollar and the U.S. dollar is merely a green piece of paper backed by nothing and redeemable in nothing. If the U.S. dollar collapses, it won't merely be a national disaster like the German Mark's collapse in the 1920's. The dollar would carry down with it the currencies of 50 or 60 other nations which use the dollar as backing for their own currency. The crash that would follow would make 'the great depression' look like a joke by comparison.

I don't know that there's enough time remaining to set up something, like the Constant Currency system, which could cushion the collapse of the free world monetary system. -But we have to act on the hopeful basis that it's not too late. All of the necessary research on indices, etc. has been done. Three things would be required. First, a group of people with banking talent. Second, a group of people with statistical talent. Third, a sufficient amount of capital to initiate operations. A minimum of $250,000 would be required, but more would make things easier. One final remark: To one who questions the idea of money backed by a spectrum, of commodities rather than just gold, I recommend John Kenneth Galbraith's new book, *Money*. Among other things, Galbraith points out that the colony of Virginia used a pound of tobacco as its monetary standard for over 150 years - a longer period of time than we had the gold standard in America."

With regard to government interference, Borsodi's words should not be taken as too much comfort. In a personal conversation that I had in 1988 with Terry Mollner, one of Borsodi's associates in the experiment, he told me that they had had a visit from the Securities and Exchange Commission just as they were closing up shop. What the SEC wanted, or just how much of a problem the government regulatory agencies would have posed, may never be known. The question was moot at that point so no one pursued it. Also, with regard to Borsodi's statement that the U.S. dollar is "backed by nothing and redeemable in nothing", something more needs to be said. While Borsodi's statement may be accepted in terms of conventional monetary thinking, it is not quite accurate. The reality is that the U.S. dollar, like all fiat currencies, is backed by force, i.e. the power of the government to tax, either directly or by its inflationary manipulation of its currency. So long as people have any confidence in it at all, and so long as alternatives remain absent, it remains redeemable in the marketplace for the wealth of the country, including the land and natural resources which, because of international exchange rate manipulations, are increasingly falling into the hands of absentee owners.

References

Bilgram, Hugo & Louis Edward Levy, *The Cause of Business Depressions*, J. B. Lippincott, Philadelphia, 1914.

Blain, Robert, "United States Public and Private Debt: 1791 to 2000", *International Social Science Journal* , UNESCO, November, 1987. Paris.

Borsodi, Ralph, *Inflation and the Coming Keynsian Catastrophe: The Story of the Exeter Experiment With Constants*, E. F. Schumacher Society, RD 3, Box 76, Great Barrington, MA 01230, 1989.

Dunkman, Wm. E., *Money, Credit and Banking*, Random House, New York, 1970.

Fisher, Irving, *Stamp Scrip,* Adelphi Company, New York, 1933.

Gesell, Silvio, *The Natural Economic Order* , 1913. English translation of the 6th. German edition, Free Economy Publishing Company, San Antonio, TX, 1934.

Homer, Sidney, *A History of Interest Rates*, Riutgers Univ. Press, 1963.

Hopman, Conrad, *Community Cooperation Coordinator,* (Text, computer programs, diskettes), B.P. 225, Noumea, New Caledonia, South Pacific.

Kinney, Mark, *A Flow Chart For Liberation: A Hypothesis of History And a Liberative Strategy For The 1990s*. New Civilization, 16255 Ventura Blvd. #605, Encino, CA 91436, 1989.

Kinney, Mark, *Global Economic Net-Dollar System*, 950 Martinsburg Road, Mt. Vernon, OH 43050, 1989.

Linton, Michael and Thomas Greco, "The Local Employment Trading System", *Whole Earth Review* , No. 55, Summer 1987, pp. 104-109.

Riegel, E. C., *Flight From Inflation: The Monetary Alternative*. The Heather Foundation, Box 48, San Pedro, CA 90733, 1978.

Siegel, Barry N. (ed.), *Money In Crisis*, Pacific Institute for Public Policy Research, San Francisco, 1984.

Zander, Walter, "A Way Out Of The Monetary Chaos", *From The Annals of Collective Economy, Geneva, 1936?*

Sources:

CRC Bulletin . Committee to Restore the Constitution, P.O. Box 986, Fort Collins, CO 80522.

E. F. Schumacher Society. RD 3, Box 76, Great Barrington, MA 01230.

The Fourth World Review. 24 Abercorn Place, London NW8, England.

Honest Money For America. 1023 South Adams St., Olympia, WA 98501.

The Local Employment and Trading System. Michael Linton, Landsman Community Services 375 Johnston Ave., Courtenay, BC V9N 2Y2 Canada.

School of Living/*Green Revolution*. RD 1, Box 185 A, Cochranville, PA 19330.